The Woman's Retirement Book

The Woman's Retirement Book

EVERYTHING YOU NEED TO KNOW NOW TO PLAN FOR THE YEARS AHEAD

Carole Sinclair

Crown Trade Paperbacks
New York

Published by Crown Publishers, Inc., 201 East 50th Street, New York,
New York 10022. Member of the Crown Publishing Group.

Random House, Inc. New York, Toronto, London, Sydney, Auckland

CROWN TRADE PAPERBACKS and colophon are trademarks of
Crown Publishers, Inc.

Manufactured in the United States of America

Library of Congress Cataloging-in-Publication Data

Sinclair, Carole.
[When women retire]
The women's retirement book : everything you need to know now
to plan for the years ahead / Carole Sinclair.—1st ed.
p.   cm.
Originally published: When women retire. 1st ed. New York : Crown
Publishers, 1992.
Includes index.
1. Women—United States—Retirement.   2. Retirement—United
States—Planning.   I. Title.
HQ1064.U5S56   1994
646.7'9—dc20   93-50227   CIP

ISBN 0-517-88171-3

10 9 8 7 6 5 4 3 2 1

First Paperback Edition

To my mother, whose retirement inspired me

Acknowledgments

I wish to express my gratitude, first and foremost, to my editor, Betty A. Prashker, who for years has been on the cutting edge of publishing for women. And special thanks to Irene Prokop for her editorial assistance and guidance.

And finally, my deep appreciation to Caroline Urbas, my second in command and sounding board, and to my daughter Wendy, who was involved in every aspect of developing this book.

To the Reader

This book is intended to provide general information. The publisher, author, and copyright owner are not engaged in rendering personal finance, investment, tax, accounting, legal, or other professional advice and services and cannot assume responsibility for individual decisions made by readers.

Should assistance for these types of advice and services be required, professionals should be consulted.

References to tax provisions in this book are based on current tax laws and regulations. Revisions in tax law, if adopted, might affect the tax consequences.

Contents

□ Part Three □

OBSTACLES IN RETIREMENT AND HOW
TO PREPARE FOR THEM

Introduction:
Why Do Women
Need This Book?

Retirement is a lot like the traditional family. Everyone has a vision of what it should be like, but only about 25 percent of the population fits the description. In general, retirement is photographically pictured as a husband and wife, both in their late fifties, physically fit and attractive, and *affluent,* enjoying themselves on a deserted Florida beach. While this is an interesting view of retirement and it is the ideal that many people expect, very few actually live it. The reasons are not entirely negative. While fully two-thirds of those who retire find they do not have enough money to cover living expenses, there are many others who retire only briefly before starting some kind of new active income-producing life because they find retirement boring or distasteful. Very few retired people actually move to a Florida beach, and of those who do, many move back to where they lived before because they miss their family and friends.

Nevertheless, retirement is a useful concept in that it clearly delineates a time that is generally the final third of one's life. This comes as a surprise to many, because they expect to retire later and don't expect to live as long, but this time span generally covers from about age fifty-five to about age eighty. The valid part of the retirement concept is that almost all people do retire from whatever it was they were doing for the twenty-five or thirty years prior to this time. Most people do retire *to* something that produces income and requires effort and involvement. For many, these are indeed golden years, not because they are free to be idle, but because they are free to do things they always wanted to do.

The traditional definition of retirement has always been based on stability—stability in the family, stability in the workplace, stability in the economy. We now live in a time of great instability—in all of these realms—and expectations during retirement have changed to reflect this. Women's lives during the last three or four decades have undergone enormous change, far greater than that reflected in men's lives. These great changes have led to a pressing need for women to plan their own retirement.

Part One

WHAT IS
RETIREMENT?

Chapter 1

Women and Retirement

❧❧❧❧

Some Things Women Are Less Likely to Do Than Men: Receive a pension (23 percent of women do; 45 percent of men do).

—TIME MAGAZINE SPECIAL ISSUE: "WOMEN, THE ROAD AHEAD," FALL 1990

HOW TRADITIONAL SCENARIOS HAVE CHANGED

Ideally, everyone would start planning for retirement upon receipt of the first paycheck, and yet the reality is that women don't begin to think about retirement until their forties and fifties. In fact, most women think about it only when jolted into it.

Yet if psychiatrists are correct that a woman's happiness is largely dependent on the amount of control she exercises over her life, then that is reason enough to plan your retirement. If you don't plan it, you will simply be forced to react to events. Control of your retirement planning and ultimate retirement may not lead to great wealth, but it could lead to your control over the decisions regarding where you live in retirement, what kind of health care you have, and how you supplement your income.

In a traditional middle-class scenario, either the wife never works outside the home or she works only sporadically or briefly and, regardless of her position in the work force, "retires" with her husband.

In the traditional male work experience, a man enters the work force in his early twenties and works his way up the ladder in possibly only one corporation or maybe two, progressively gaining increases in salary, title, and responsibility.

....

Women can, and should, control their own retirement.

....

During this work experience, the man benefits from corporate health plans, possibly profit sharing, and possibly a pension (currently, 45 percent of all American men collect a pension). Standard retirement age has been sixty-five, although that has gradually been moving back to earlier ages, with a fairly large number of men retiring in their late fifties. The pension awaiting these men can be taken in a lump sum or paid out over the retiree's remaining years.

Upon retirement, this middle-class male also begins collecting Social Security payments and benefiting from Medicare. When the life span for the average American male was seventy or under, this worked out nicely and the widow would continue to receive pension benefits, Social Security benefits, life insurance proceeds, and an almost certain profit on the family home.

Since the 1960s, in one short generation, everything has changed.

Most young women enter the work force now as soon as they complete their education. According to a recent newspaper article, 60 percent of those who entered their first marriages in the 1980s will be divorced. The figures are higher for second and third marriages.

In a divorce the woman no longer automatically gets the kids, the house, and lifetime alimony. In fact, she may not get any of that. On top of this reality, she will almost certainly incur fairly steep legal bills to disengage herself from her marriage.

There are also increasing numbers of women who choose never to marry. Recent surveys indicate that they like their single status and maintain it by choice. Single women are far happier than single men, and at least as happy as married women. These single women have always been on their own financially, and tend to be much better off financially than women leaving marriages, women in bad marriages, and even many women in workable marriages.

Regardless of one's marital or social status, men cannot necessarily be depended upon anymore in retirement. First of all, that traditional male work experience has changed to one that now includes downsizing, layoffs, firings, loss of health benefits, and loss of retirement benefits. When this instability in male financial status is combined with a longer life span for both men and women, new contingency plans need to be made by women.

....

The concept of retirement has taken on a new meaning.

....

Into this complicated situation, one must factor two incidents that are on the increase: the financial dependence of parents upon their retired children, and children forced to return home to live because of the shrinking job market and high cost of housing.

Moreover, the barrier of mandatory retirement age is being eliminated and many of those in retirement are finding they can't pay their bills and/or are bored and unhappy.

Because of all these factors, we are faced with the possibility that the long-cherished notion of retirement might be considered a quaint, totally outmoded concept in another twenty or thirty years.

This raises the whole question of whether retirement is even a workable idea. In many other developed countries, such as Japan, people in good health *never* retire, they simply cut back their working hours and take on less-demanding roles in whatever their business is. They gradually increase the amount of vacation they have but never really become unproductive, and they rarely become a burden on society.

This all sounds terrific, and yet we have an American corporate environment that is very youth oriented and oftentimes views executives over fifty with some suspicion.

But then, of course, our economy is currently in shambles, and perhaps this long-accepted process of gradually phasing out workers in their fifties will, out of necessity, give way to one whereby people in their fifties and sixties and even seventies are more highly valued and utilized because of their experience and wisdom.

The over-fifty segment of the population is a political powerhouse. Older people vote, older people join the American Association of Retired Persons (AARP), and older people control the bulk of the wealth in this country. In fact, some major think tanks offer the prospect of a scenario in which this group looks out for itself and basically freezes out people now in their twenties and thirties trying to make their way through the corporation at middle-management levels.

This would be a mixed blessing. On the one hand, it would be beneficial to our economy to have people in their fifties, sixties, and seventies gainfully employed and not dependent on public assistance. It would also be very handy to have them contributing to Social Security. On the other hand, while the younger people have no real desire to carry a disproportionate amount of the burden of supporting able-bodied people over fifty who are in retirement, they also do not wish to be dead-ended in their careers. People in the work force in their twenties and thirties right now are highly motivated, have come out of the super-optimistic Eighties, and are psychologically ill prepared for anything other than upward mobility.

Where do these changing scenarios leave women who want to plan for retirement?

Most probably on their own, out on a limb, without a safety net, without role models, and without much help from the government. Only about 23 percent of all women who work right now ever collect any kind of a pension. Large numbers of elderly women live below the poverty level.

Even women who have worked a number of years tend to be the first victims of downsizing and layoffs (eliminated before their male counterparts) in any kind of economic slump such as the one we're in now.

....

If a job gives your life structure, plan to replace that structure in retirement.

....

Women face the same psychological trauma as men who lose their jobs. They have come to depend on the structure it gives their lives, the income and cash flow, the benefits, the promise of a bright future, the sense of self-worth, and pure physical accomplishment. In addition, the workplace offers camaraderie, involvement, and—for women at middle and upper levels of management—access to support staff and services. These women have become efficient delegators and are accustomed to operating from the base of their employment. This experience impacts how they manage their day-to-day life, the way they raise their children, and, of extreme importance, how they conduct their social lives. It is also likely to impact their standard of living, travel mobility, educational advancement and opportunity, and health—both mental and physical.

Women who unexpectedly lose their jobs are depressed, vulnerable, economically endangered, and socially afloat.

Younger and middle-aged women in the work force often define themselves in terms of their jobs. Although the outside world may still define them in terms of their marriages and children, they tend to think of themselves foremost as professional, working individuals.

Many women who have tried both prefer to be at the office rather than at home. It's more manageable, there's more help, it's more rational, the quality of people you deal with is higher, it has a paycheck, it has definition, it has a future. Very few women who lose their jobs have any desire to become full-time homemakers again.

Even in the best of all circumstances where a woman is comfortably retired, either on her husband's benefits or on her own, there can be another kind of bleak scenario. Every day there are headlines questioning whether Social Security will survive or continue to exist at all in its current form. Politicians vow that Social Security funds are inviolate and will not be disturbed for any reason, but with the national deficit looming, there are those who feel Social Security is in grave danger.

More frightening are the headlines questioning the strength of major insurance companies that have been weakened recently by the slump in junk bonds and in real estate, in which many are heavily invested, as well as by the big cost of the AIDS epidemic. Any weakness in these companies could conceivably affect their ability to pay on life insurance policies, disability policies, and annuities. This would adversely influence even the most well-thought-out retirement plans.

The collapse of several savings and loan institutions has already adversely affected the retirement of thousands. Even though there is a government bailout plan, taxpayers are footing the enormous cost in the form of additional taxes.

The FDIC (Federal Deposit Insurance Corporation) insures individual bank accounts up to $100,000, but bank failures in the New York area alone have wiped out portions of people's savings in excess of that amount. Many banks are weakened primarily from bad real-estate loans during the 1980s and represent, at this point, some risk to depositors.

Chapter 2

Married Women
and Retirement

~~~~~

*Poverty Looms for Many Women Who Take Time
Off from Jobs*

*Many women can't count on husbands to help at retire-
ment time. Forty percent of women are single when they
retire.*

*Currently half as many women receive pensions as
men, and those that do get paid only two-thirds as
much. That helps explain why 41 percent of women over
sixty-five are poor or near poor, compared with 17 percent of men. The Washington-based Older Women's
League backs legislation sponsored by Representative William Hughes of New Jersey to give women credit with
Social Security for caring for children or old people.*

—THE WALL STREET JOURNAL, FEBRUARY 5, 1991

PLANNING SEPARATELY FROM
YOUR SPOUSE

If you are married, even happily or at least permanently married, you need to think about your retirement—as
separate from your husband's retirement.

First of all, there is a 50 percent chance you will become divorced. That percentage becomes even higher if this is your second or third marriage.

There is also more than a 50 percent chance that you will be widowed. If your husband is under age sixty-five, the chances are greater that he will be disabled than that he will die.

Corporate America is no longer a stable and predictable place. No matter what your husband's employment situation, there is no certainty that he will remain employed there or even that his employer will stay in business. The chances are good that your husband's company will be caught up in downsizing, a merger, or even a bankruptcy. The American economy is weak, and corporate structures are all vulnerable.

If you have never worked outside of the home, or have worked only part time or at volunteer work, you are entirely dependent on your husband's pension, profit sharing, income, health insurance, disability insurance, and life insurance.

....

Even married women should develop their own retirement strategy.

....

As the profitability of American corporations has declined in the face of world competition, most companies have taken a serious look at the cost of maintaining their benefit programs.

A generation ago, these benefit programs might have been equal to 10 percent of the cost of maintaining an employee. Now it's more likely to be somewhere between 25 percent and 35 percent of that cost. One of the main reasons is the out-of-control cost of health care. When your husband joined his company, he may have had 100 percent, or certainly 80 percent or 90 percent, coverage of all health-care costs. Now it is more likely that a maximum of 80 percent of health-care costs are covered, and he is making a significant contribution to the cost of the corporate health insurance. Moreover, he is probably under some restrictions about the use of private doctors, new procedures, and certain medications. He may have no coverage, for instance, unless he uses the services of an HMO (Health Maintenance Organization). Or he may have no coverage for psychological treatment.

Unfortunately, you can only expect this situation to get worse. As long as health care is a private matter in America and there is no national health insurance, corporations will view it as a fixed expense and a legitimate target for cost cutting and efficiency campaigns. Even more ominous, health benefits extended to employee and spouse at the same level after retirement as during the individual's working years may soon be a thing of the past. Corporations are just beginning to experiment with sharply reducing health benefits for retirees. Many early-retirement packages, which offer an attractive lump sum up front, do so at the expense of health-care coverage later in life.

Pension plans, which were once adequate to cover living expenses after retirement, are also on shaky ground. Although pensions and their funding and structure are partially protected by the Pension Benefit Guarantee Corporation, the health-care benefits of individual companies cannot be legislated. When a company fails, goes out of business, declares bankruptcy, is acquired by a foreign buyer, or becomes involved in litigation because of mismanagement, all employees suffer, particularly those who were planning on vested funds to provide a comfortable retirement.

When you combine the instability of the structure of corporate America, our shaky economy, the out-of-control costs of health care, and, finally, increased longevity, you have a potential disaster for very large numbers of people. Pension and health-care programs were originally structured, generations ago, when life expectancy was perhaps seventy years. Now that that has changed to seventy-five, eighty, eighty-five, and longer, these plans are hopelessly inadequate.

It is simply prudent for married women to assume responsibility for their own retirement. The ideal situation is for them to work in conjunction with their husbands in their planning and to develop retirement plans of their own as well. No one complains when there is too much money in retirement or too much health-care insurance or too much life insurance.

ACHIEVING FINANCIAL INDEPENDENCE

If you are married and have fulfilled the traditional role of wife, mother, homemaker, perhaps community volunteer, you can think about and plan for your retirement without making any major change in your lifestyle.

Because there is always the chance, in fact a good chance, that you will have to cover some and perhaps even all of your expenses in retirement, you could begin by looking at your insurance needs. Even if your husband is covered by a health-care policy at work, look into obtaining your own health insurance, perhaps a modest policy tied to an HMO. With such a policy, you will still have the flexibility and the freedom of using your own doctors and having your bills paid by your husband's insurance. Should his coverage end, however, you will have a backup that will "break your fall." In other words, although the HMO might require that you use their physicians and make appointments weeks or months in advance, and while they may restrict you on some procedures, at least you will not be left completely vulnerable. The cost of such an HMO policy is relatively modest compared to other private health insurance and it would give you peace of mind as well as an important protection, even if you never need it.

Although you may feel that your husband's pension plus Social Security payments will be sufficient to fund your retirement, I suggest that you set up a small, separate fund anyway as a hedge. You could start an IRA with $2,000 a year, or a Keogh if you qualify, or you could purchase a small annuity through an insurance company. You'll find that the impact of steady savings and compounded interest and tax deferral will produce a very sizable nest egg after ten, twenty, or thirty years. And it will be there, safe, in your name, when you need it.

You may feel that your housing needs are covered because you and your husband own your own home and it's almost or completely paid for. You're wrong. If you or your husband run into financial or health difficulties, the first thing to go could be the house. It is probably your largest asset and it is relatively liquid. It is also your best option for borrowing, even if you do not sell it. You could find yourself, at age fifty, seeking work and taking out a substantial mortgage. (The special needs of homemakers with children will be discussed in a later chapter.) Unfortunately, in today's housing market, the house may not rise appreciably in value over the next five or seven years. While making mortgage payments with your husband may be doable, making them without him might be impossible and you could find yourself losing your house. Moreover, if you've borrowed against your house using a home equity loan and you are unable to make the payments, you *will* lose your home.

Look into the possibility of investment housing in your own name. Remember that your retirement planning is meant to put a floor under you and prevent a disaster. Don't look at six-bedroom houses on rolling green lawns. Rather, look to purchase perhaps a one-bedroom condominium, or a "cottage," or even a multiple-dwelling rental property. Once you make the down payment, your plans should be to rent out this real estate to cover your expenses and, if you are fortunate, to show a small profit. It's simply there, like your HMO and IRA, when you need it. And, if financial misfortune strikes, this property can be sold to produce immediate cash.

If you've read the previous pages, you may be saying to yourself, "She's right, I should do all of those things, and I would, except I don't have my own money." Nonsense. Of course you have your "own money." Even if you are in a situation where your husband is the only source of income and he provides you with some sort of monthly allowance to run the household, buy clothes, pay the bills, and plan trips, you can begin to save a portion of that money. It is not difficult to set aside enough money to cover an HMO. A small savings account, perhaps a money market fund, can be started on relatively little. The point in both cases is simply to get started. Buying real estate, on the other hand, is obviously going to require some kind of down payment, even if it is modest.

I strongly recommend that every married woman have some activity that produces some income of her own. There are endless opportunities, and surely there's one in a field that would appeal to you or in which you have some expertise. These opportunities for generating income could include part-time or substitute teaching, selling real estate, working in a retail establishment, doing telemarketing at home for a corporation, or—my favorite—starting a small business. It is certainly worth doing one of these things even for a few hours a week so you can begin to generate a little money for investment. If you take these steps, even in your forties, you will find that by the time you are sixty or seventy, you have in place a workable emergency contingency fund. Remember that the sooner you start, the more options will be open to you.

Chapter 3

Retirement and the New Woman

૯૦૦૦૦

The "corporate wife" must be distinguished from the corporate "wife." In the first case the woman is married to a spouse and his corporation, and in the second she is married to her *own* corporation. This represents a strange sort of progress in my opinion. A generation or two ago, young women aspired to being "corporate wives." They were prepared to fulfill the role of wife, mother, homemaker, and assistant to the husband in all matters regarding his corporation. While that sort of life appears to have gone out of vogue, it has been replaced by the corporate "wife," or the "new woman."

Droves of young women, upon graduating from college and/or graduate school, throw themselves into corporate-oriented lives. Many of them have a child or several children and a husband or a succession of husbands. Throughout it all, their focus remains on their own corporate identity. A generation of these women is now nearing retirement age. The general consensus seems to be that the corporations have offered them many opportunities and enriched them financially and mentally. What they are learning, however, is that their corporations are not going to do any more for them than they did for their fathers or husbands or male colleagues. Interestingly, while many of these women have been buffeted by child-custody battles, the empty-nest syndrome, and lackluster marriages, they have derived mental, intellectual, financial, and social structure—and security— from their corporations. These corporate women have even been much envied by their more traditional stay-at-home female counterparts. As they reach their forties and fifties, however, many of them, like the men before them, are unprepared for the shock of life after the corporation. Some of these women will simply put off the issue until they retire or are forcibly retired. Those women will suffer the greatest shock when their corporate identity is summarily yanked out from under them. They will find their financial situation much reduced and restricted, and they will be unprepared for the anxiety and uncertainty of having to be responsible for, or at least supplement, the many benefits they have come to take for granted, primarily their paycheck and health insurance coverage.

••

The corporate "wife" must consider special issues when planning for retirement.

••

Most women in their twenties and thirties spend little or no time thinking about their retirement or even life with-

Professional and Trade Organizations

While you may have grown to find the activities of your professional or trade organization boring, repetitive, even petty, and while such organizations may seem to benefit the younger members more than others, it's worth taking another look. Such organizations and the activities they sponsor are excellent for helping you keep on top of what's going on at your competitors and in related fields. Stick with it and sooner or later something worthwhile will come of it. Remember, your objective is to lay a new and somewhat more independent plan for your next ten, twenty, or thirty working years. Be open to new ideas.

Separate—But Still Involved

Although it is certainly advisable to plan for the day when you will have no identity with your current corporation and corporate network, the ideal situation is still one in which you stay involved with them in some way.

....

Avoid the physical and mental traps in retirement, too.

....

The perfect solution is to continue to work for your corporation either on a part-time basis or as a consultant or supplier or adviser. This would permit you to have the all-important name identification as well as at least some of the perks. You might even be able to orchestrate a situation whereby you continue to have a corporate title of some sort as well as office space, secretarial help, some health and insurance benefits. While such deals are rare, they can be worked out with careful planning—even manipulation.

If you are one of those people who feel that you are valuable because the XYZ Corporation says you are and has made you a vice president, you need to work a bit on your own self-image. Keep in mind that corporations are not charities and they wouldn't have given you the vice presidency if you didn't perform a useful service and ultimately contribute to their bottom line. If you can do it at the XYZ Corporation, you can do it elsewhere, either at another corporation, at a university, or in your own business.

Health Caution

Even if you were an athlete in college and perhaps physically very active in your twenties, you may since have married, had one or more children, and settled into a relatively comfortable corporate existence. Beware. Your energy level may be dangerously low. The task ahead of you will require high energy and good health. While you probably took energy and health for granted in your twenties and thirties, you can't do that in your forties. And you most certainly can't do it in your fifties, sixties, and seventies. If you start now, as you plan to reshape your professional life, to also reshape your physical self into one that is healthier and more active and more capable, you will have greater success on your professional front and put off the assorted physical and mental traps that await you in these next decades.

YOUR FLUCTUATING NEEDS

Perhaps you have given a great deal to your corporation and your corporation has given a great deal to you—in fact, everything you felt you needed professionally for twenty or thirty years. Even so, don't be trapped into thinking that the corporation can necessarily meet your needs in your fifties, sixties, or seventies. Your needs are different then. If, for instance, you work in advertising and have been the hotshot female vice president in your division from age thirty-two to forty-two, you have to realize that your advertising agency might not offer you much in your fifties. Perhaps the corporate environment is very pro-youth and very anti-middle-age. Why put up with it? Unless you own the agency and can change it in your lifetime, perhaps you'd be happier to turn fifty in politics! While advertising might view you as useless at fifty-five or sixty, state politics thinks you are just beginning to come into your own now. Men, and interestingly women, are viewed as young if they are in politics at age fifty. They are viewed as experienced at sixty and seasoned at sixty-five. Increasingly, politicians in their seventies think nothing of running for local, state, and even national office.

If in your thirties you got a major thrill from working on Wall Street (even if it was fourteen hours a day, including Saturdays, and meant never seeing your friends, family, or much of anything but your job), you may find that, no matter what they call you or what they pay you, you simply don't want to do that in your fifties. If your objective is more time, no commute, better climate, less stress, then you will probably be *better* able to meet your needs out of your current corporation. Don't delude yourself with thinking that what made you happy in one decade will necessarily make you happy in another. Try to get a realistic fix on what you are going to want in later decades and don't become unnecessarily glum over losing something that would be only a major hassle to you at a later age.

In short, don't lament the potential loss of your corporation if your corporation won't be in any position to deliver what you need later in life. Chances are that your sense of well-being depends on feeling productive, useful, involved, important. The trick is to steer yourself to an activity that provides the income you need with this kind of mental stimulation and satisfaction.

Let's assume you're forty, have worked ever since you left college or graduate school, have perhaps been married once or twice and had one or more children, and perhaps you are still married. Through it all, you *always* worked full time and have reached a level where you in fact make more money than your current husband and have for years paid 60 percent to 70 percent of the costs of caring for your child or children. You are indeed Superwoman! On top of this, you probably find your professional life enormously satisfying and take more than a little pleasure in the income level you have achieved. You are certainly to be congratulated.

And yet there is a flip side to this sunny scenario. In your retirement, not only are you likely to be entirely responsible for yourself and your expenses, but since you have long carried the family and household, chances are you will be expected to continue to do the same. If, like many professional women who have achieved your stature, you had children late, as you enter your fifties and sixties you may well just be beginning to pay the cost of college and graduate school and even early living expenses and "getting settled" expenses for your children.

If you have long brought in a higher income than your husband, perhaps you are the one with the corporate existence and perhaps he is a teacher, or freelance writer, or musician, or works in some other profession that does not come with perks, high salaries, a pension, profit sharing, and extensive health, disability, and life insurance. If you are both approximately the same age, he will see his modest income diminish long before you will see yours diminish. There will be a great deal of pressure on you to not even think about retirement in your fifties, and maybe not even in your sixties.

This is not all bad. Chances are you will be happier, and

physically and mentally healthier, if you continue to perform and get credit for your professional existence.

The important reason to face this is you may be part of a group of personal friends who have a certain mind-set about turning fifty-five or sixty. Your friends may talk endlessly of golf courses, beaches, travel. This will not be for you—but then, you may already get all of the travel, golf courses, and beaches you want and need as corporate perks!

....

Your personal definition of retirement can help you shape the future.

....

Not everyone waits to be "retired." For many people, retirement is something they will personally control and orchestrate and time. A good example is a woman who lives in my cooperative apartment building. When I was applying to purchase my apartment, it was suggested that I meet with several members of the co-op board, and hers was one of the names I was given. I was told she was "retired." I quickly envisioned the usual stereotype of someone sixty-five and at home. I made an appointment to see her, and when I arrived at her apartment, I was rather amazed to find that she was certainly not sixty-five, and probably closer to thirty-five. I told her immediately that I had been told she was "retired" and I was surprised to meet her. She just laughed and said she *was* retired and that she had retired when she wanted to, at age thirty-five. She went on to explain that she had been a trainee and then a broker in one of the major high-power Wall Street firms. She had put in more than ten years of fourteen-hour days, six or seven days a week, but apparently not to buy Fendi pocketbooks and BMWs. Instead, she saved every penny she could and simply set her retirement-age goal at thirty-five rather than, say, fifty-five. At thirty-five she did indeed retire, and when I met her she was fulfilling a lifetime dream of working as a full-time painter and water-colorist. She confirmed that yes, she had earned, saved, and invested enough during her years on Wall Street to fund her current comfortable lifestyle. Apparently her husband had taken a dim view of her retirement plan, though, and they were now divorced. I met her five years ago and she has just remarried. She told me recently that she has now "retired" from painting and has moved to Connecticut with her new husband and stepchildren and has opened a small retail business, using funds she set aside years ago. She is now in her early forties, and I must say I will be very interested to see what she's doing in her fifties, in her sixties, in her seventies . . . and on.

Chapter 4

The Stages of Retirement

~~~~~

Your Money . . . A Longer Life and Saving for It

*Americans are on a collision course with an economic
reality, living longer, retiring earlier and saving less
than they did a generation ago.*
   *Beginning early in the next century America may face
widespread indigence, or poverty among the elderly.*

       —NEW YORK TIMES, SEPTEMBER 28, 1991

You know, without question, that your twenties,
thirties, and forties have been very distinctive decades. Your
economic, social, professional, and even health scenario has
been dramatically different in each of those three decades.
    Retirement will be the same. Your fifties, sixties, seven-
ties, eighties, and later are again each dramatically different
decades. For some people, the fifties bring early retirement,
children leaving home, the end of college expenses, and the
onset of minor health problems. For many other people, the
fifties represent peaking professionally, economically, and
frequently psychologically. The sixties, regardless of how
you feel personally and physically, bring the technical nationally recognized retirement decade, and yet for increasingly large numbers of working men and women, all of this
propaganda is largely ignored and they continue to try to
move ahead with a continuation of their fifties.
    These early-retirement years, of the fifties and sixties,

will probably find you not retired at all. Very few people, especially women, have the financial resources to close down their gainful employment and complementing lifestyle to embark on three decades of leisure. This period of the fifties and sixties does, however, in almost all cases bring on some kind of change in one's professional status, frequently a move to self-employment or part-time employment. Although during the entire time you may be bombarded with endless pieces in your mailbox and commercials on TV showing handsome, fit, inevitably gray-haired men and women frolicking in their retirement, there are very few people in their age bracket who actually look this way or live this way.

All of the social, physical, employment, and personal changes we generally associate with this early-retirement phase actually happen in the second phase of retirement, which may start sometime in your late sixties and continue through your seventies. This is a time when you may in fact cease most, but not all, gainful employment. You probably will be burdened with a number of minor to not-so-minor health problems. At this age, your financial obligation to your children may be over, but you may have the new difficulty of your own elderly parents and perhaps an ailing spouse.

Unless you have planned very carefully on the financial front, this can be a disappointing and exhausting time, since at the same time you will not be able to perform at the peaks you achieved in your fifties and sixties, you may be faced with fifteen or more years of retirement and therefore be ill equipped to handle it. Although you may have thought during your thirties and forties that you were aiming to retire at fifty-five or sixty, chances are it's more likely to be in your early seventies or later. During this time a smaller home, better climate, proximity to friends and medical facilities all become very real needs, but if these needs are to be fulfilled, you will have needed to have done the research and laid the groundwork for this in your fifties and sixties.

A third stage of your retirement, your eighties and thereafter, will hopefully find you in good physical condition and economically comfortable. It is realistic to plan, however, for increased medical expenses, some diminishing in your physical ability, and dependence on medical facilities and family members.

The important thing to remember is that these three cycles of your retirement may run more years than your total years of employment. As a woman, the chances of this are *great*. Most women, even those who enter the work force immediately upon graduation from college or graduate school, do take time off throughout their careers for bearing and raising children, meeting the needs of a spouse, and increasingly meeting the needs of elderly parents. Where this leaves you is facing possibly three decades of so-called retirement on the financial floor you've been able to put under yourself in perhaps only twenty years.

The solution, of course, is to plan, research, save, and spread your risk, just like in your investments. Don't bank on a spouse, Social Security, a partial pension, or investments to carry the entire financial burden for you. Plan early to further spread your sources of income during retirement, thereby opening up for yourself the option of earning more income than you even now feel you might need.

Such structuring, planning, and researching provides a tremendous boost psychologically. It gives you control, optimism, *and* pleasure.

TYPES OF RETIREMENT AND ARE THEY FOR YOU?

Retirement is allegedly when you stop your full-time work, career, profession, or labor and enjoy a life of leisure or whatever you choose. Financial difficulties are eliminated for you because you have funded your retirement during your years of employment.

There actually are men who do retire under these circumstances, but few, if any, women manage this. The main reason for the difficulty lies in the multiplicity of roles in the average woman's life. Women have traditionally cared for children, aging parents, and, if married, spouses. Even if the husband, or the companion of one's choice, is off at the golf course, the chances are excellent that the woman continues to juggle management of the home, crises in the life of teenagers and even adult children, and any health care that needs to be provided at home for aging parents and in some cases other relatives.

···

Each stage of retirement has special requirements.

···

Consequently, retirement for women is at best partial. The fortunate ones do retire from their employment with pensions (23 percent of working women receive a pension), as well as benefits from investments, insurance, real estate, and Social Security. Retirement from their other roles, however, is generally impossible, but as with everything else in life, a well-laid long-range plan can ease later burdens and aggravation.

The Leisure Option

Although this book comes down very hard on the issue of money, your need for it, and your need to provide for it for yourself, I do want to touch on the option of a retirement of leisure.

As I've already pointed out, for women with husbands, grown children at home, or aging parents at home, retirement is an elusive thing. For the very large number of women who retire alone, however, the leisure option is viable. Some women, like men, can't wait for their sixty-fifth birthday, when they get to leave their longtime employment, collect Social Security, and become eligible for Medicare and a wide array of senior discounts.

Wide-ranging research indicates that women, like their male counterparts, are more eager to leave their employment if they have been at a middle or lower level, with little control over their days and activities, and with limited intellectual stimulation. On the other hand, women in top positions in corporate life, academia, and the professions have much less desire to leave what is for them a stimulating, rewarding, lucrative, and sometimes luxurious existence.

Since there are more people in the middle and at the bottom than at the top, however, their concerns are more widespread. For women who are alone and look forward to their retirement and walking away from the employed life they have known, the leisure option is viable and in fact a desirable one. The issue becomes money. Although it is assumed that you will need 70 percent of your current income to fund your retirement years, that is simply an average. If you would be willing to live on much less, in a new location, rather than continuing some kind of employment, then you should plan for that scenario.

If you are perhaps a mid-level employee at a major manufacturer in a major metropolitan area, it may be your goal to leave that metropolitan area as soon as possible and to seek beaches, mountains, or woods. The key thing for you is to draw up a budget for yourself that covers all important essentials such as your contingency fund, proper health insurance, and housing. Perhaps you've decided you can do without the lifestyle and costs of a metropolitan area. Perhaps you are slashing from your budget a new car, new clothes, travel, eating out, entertainment, and instead you are investing everything you have (eventually including the money you clear on the sale of your home) in such a way as to provide only one-third or one-half of your previous income. Perhaps you can piece this together when you add in Social Security and any kind of corporate retirement benefits you will receive. If you control your own life and you are independent and healthy, this can be a very exciting scenario. If you choose your new geographic location with great care, watching such items as the general cost of living, cost of real estate, and taxes, and if you plan carefully down to the last penny, you should be able to pull it off.

Several years ago, while traveling to a particularly remote and beautiful Caribbean island, I had a chance to meet the only American in residence year round on this tiny, remarkable island, a retired college professor from Boston. She had been looking forward to this kind of retirement all of her life, and she assured me that she did not miss the academic and social stimulation of a city like Boston, nor did she miss all of the luxuries and conveniences to which she had grown accustomed. This woman was living on very little annual income on this island in a small, charming private house. She had been retired there for fifteen years when I met her and was something of a local legend. She spent most of her free time gardening and writing, sometimes for publication. She told me that she also taught part time at the only school on the island. I assumed this was to increase her annual income, but she pointed out that she worked only as a volunteer. She had learned to live on the money that was available, she had planned well, invested well, and knew her own mind. It is also important to note that she had vacationed on this island for more than ten years before moving there. As I marveled at what she had managed, it occurred to me that she had no need for a car, no need for heating fuel, no need for a serious wardrobe. Her health appeared to be excellent. She walked everywhere and was in wonderful physical condition. I could only guess at her age, but it would have to have been close to eighty!

The Non-Retirement Option

Let's say you are sixty-five and retiring from a senior vice presidency at your economically healthy and strong corporation. You have worked most of your career at this corporation. You are one of the fortunate ones getting a pension and possibly even profit sharing. You have no children, or your children are all living happily and independently. You have no dependent parents or relatives. You have either no husband or one who is healthy, nondependent, and enjoying his own funded retirement. Even if you are in this fortunate and most unusual situation, you have to address the question of whether you *want* to retire, whether it will make you happy, whether it's a good idea, and whether you can do anything about it.

Many important national surveys, including those done by the American Association of Retired Persons, have uncovered some interesting findings indicating that many people don't wish to retire at all. They thrive on the intellectual stimulation of their jobs and the economic freedom it gives them. Those who are forcibly retired, or who take an early retirement and regret it, frequently find that their mental and physical health deteriorates in their "life of leisure." They are unstimulated, and they become depressed and out of touch.

Many retirees who have headed south to warmer climates report that they are lonely and feel seriously disconnected from their families, especially children and grandchildren. Many end up moving back to their hometowns.

....

A true analysis of your retirement needs is fundamental.

....

If you are sixty-five and have a life expectancy of close to eighty-five, do you really want to go to the beach for twenty years?

If you are active, healthy, productive, and make a major contribution at your company, you can fight retirement. Mandatory retirement ages will probably be entirely phased out in the next several years or decade anyway, because Congress is under enormous pressure from the well-organized, articulate, wealthy over-fifty lobby.

WHAT DO YOU NEED IN RETIREMENT?

Since retirement is as much a case of having to do without things you've depended on as getting rid of things you wanted to eliminate, it is important to address both areas. First, let's look at your needs. They will include:

• *Income.* To support your lifestyle and pay your bills, you must estimate the income you will need in retirement. The rule of thumb is that you need two-thirds of your current income to maintain your current lifestyle.

• *Excellent Health Care and Proper Insurance.* This is an expense that continues to grow dramatically after age fifty. If you've had good coverage through your employment, you have the option of converting it, which will be much more expensive on an individual basis, and paying it yourself. Don't forget to factor that into your required income figure.

• *Housing.* Think long and hard about whether you want to move out of your longtime primary residence. On the one hand, you may have ten rooms and find you need only four now. Or perhaps you're tired of the high heating bill, the maintenance cost on a big lawn, or high local taxes.

On the other hand, as already mentioned, many people who move away wish they hadn't and eventually return. While a small condominium in St. Petersburg or San Diego might sound appealing, once there you may get tired of the heat, bored with being surrounded by only one age group, and feel confined in a small space. To make up for the lack of proximity to friends and family, you may wish to have a lot of company. If you have no space, however, it will be difficult to accommodate guests. And if you've moved *too* far away, many people will not be willing to incur the time or expense to visit. You may find instead that staying where you are, maintaining family and community ties and a sense of place, is more important to you. Perhaps you should have your home inspected to increase energy efficiency. Maybe you should plant ground cover where you now have grass. Maybe you should even close off a portion of your house or use it as a home office.

The reality is that, even if you should decide to move, you could have trouble finding a buyer at this time, and even if you do find a buyer, because the real-estate market is depressed, you might not clear enough profit to cover the expense of not only a move but a total relocation.

• *A Safety Net.* A hedge against unpredictable and uncontrollable events that could eliminate some of the benefits you expect from retirement is essential. Social Security, which was never meant to cover all of your expenses anyway, could play a diminishing role in your financial life. The health insurance coverage you've been enjoying could (especially if it's through a former employer) be cut way back or eliminated altogether. Dependence on funds from others is always risky, no matter how long term the relationship. The divorce figures, for instance, for those over fifty are growing at an enormous rate. (For more information on maintaining your safety net, see Section Three.)

Socially, the combination of ageism and sexism experienced by women in their sixties, seventies, and eighties can be surprisingly difficult to manage. While older men may be considered in their prime, physically attractive, marriageable, women of the same age can find themselves considered to be quite the reverse. (I am not factoring in here the new and truly amazing discovery that we can all apparently get pregnant at sixty now. Sociologists will have a field day sorting this out.) Nevertheless, just as women have to plan for income, health care, and housing, they need to lay a social plan. Isolation is dangerous, mentally and physically.

One healthy trend I see is the substantial number of older women entering politics. They are having a good time and quite a lot of success. They have figured out that there are more women their age than men, and that they indeed have a natural franchise. They have discovered that taking action and wielding power in middle age and later is an appealing idea.

Happily, for people facing retirement in the near future, the population is aging. Soon, one-third of the population will be over fifty. These people have a lot of clout. They vote. The strength in numbers that this affords should very positively impact the lives of women in retirement.

Chapter 5

Retiring onto Something:

A New Concept

～～～～

Once women have managed to cover their most basic needs in retirement, they can address their ancillary needs. For women who have worked productively and successfully and who have controlled their own lives and produced something of consequence, the worst part of retirement is loss of identity, status, center.

Women who define their lives in terms of professional achievement and standing may need to retire onto something else. This "something else" can take many forms, including high-level volunteer work, consulting, writing, teaching, and starting one's own business.

In order for you to retire onto something when you leave your current occupational slot, the groundwork needs to be laid early, preferably at about age fifty.

Your first step should be to assess your own field. Do you work in a field where age and experience are valued, or in one, such as advertising or modeling, where age is looked upon with suspicion and dread? It is not too late to take your marketable skills and move yourself to a profession where you'll have greater longevity.

Your first reaction to this advice might be that you only know how to do "whatever." You're wrong. If you have supervised a staff, managed a budget, developed a product, sold a product, spoken publicly, or written copy, you have a skill that is readily transferable. Yes, you might need to enter your new field at a somewhat lower level (though not necessarily much lower). And yes, you may need additional formal education to reach important levels. If, for instance, you move into the health-care field, or almost any other that benefits from the population's aging, you will find many opportunities to use your skills, as well as companies willing to finance any additional formal training you need. Because many of these are new industries or fast-growing ones in need of experience and expertise, you, as an older worker, will find a much warmer reception than you might in, say, TV production.

Or you may feel you'd rather take your chances where you are, even if it's obvious to you that older workers are not necessarily valued or retained. You may get lucky and things will work out for you, but you owe it to yourself to seriously consider and prepare for alternatives since the workplace is by its nature unstable.

Industries with the greatest growth, the highest salaries, the brightest future in the 1980s (such as financial services) have already been among the hardest hit in the 1990s. There have been major bankruptcies, mergers, downsizing, lay-offs. No one in the Eighties would have predicted this. Whatever it is you are involved with is vulnerable. Open up some options for yourself.

Even some professionals, such as lawyers, doctors, and dentists, who feel immune to these difficulties could be in for a surprise. Law firms have been known to ease out senior partners and to lay off recently hired associates. Patients sometimes prefer the services of a younger doctor. Clients might want the newest "young" thinking on their personal and financial matters and investing. No one is immune. *Everyone* should have a backup plan.

It makes sense to trade off of what you already know and what you're already good at. Perhaps you can arrange to do some writing, some speaking, teach part time at a local university, and, in the best of all possible cases, consult for your former employer and even his competitors.

....

Backup plans are essential for the retiree.

....

The near-perfect scenario is one where you set up a consulting arrangement with your current employer that will run five or ten years after your retirement, giving you access to an office, phone, photocopy machine, fax, secretarial help, and contacts. In so doing, you provide a service similar to the one you used to provide full time for perhaps one-half or one-third of the expense, but you're under no obligation to be at the office five days a week, to travel when you don't want to, to dress for the business world, to commute. With the advent of computers, fax machines, and Federal Express, consulting can be done easily from a home office, possibly from the extra room or rooms you felt you didn't need. Let's explore the options of retiring onto something.

START YOUR OWN BUSINESS

When all retirement activity options are considered, the one I find to offer possibly the greatest reward is starting and owning one's own business. It really has everything going for it. You own it, you're the president, you're in charge. You have status, you may have a staff. Presumably it's in an area where you have great expertise or interest. You are not dependent on anyone, you don't work for anyone, the day-to-day hassles are of your own making rather than someone else's.

If you start your own business, the chances are great that it will be in the service sector rather than manufacturing. Manufacturing involves the cost of production, maintaining inventory, shipping, patents, plant and warehouse costs. Involvement in manufacturing means money up front, either yours or money you've raised. There is great risk. You can't get into manufacturing on a small basis. Raising outside money is always difficult, but especially in our current economy. Risking your own money is questionable as well unless money is truly not an issue with you.

There are many advantages to starting a business that provides a service. First of all, if it is your personal services or those of others, you can either do it on your own or hire all free-lance help. This means you don't have the overhead of maintaining a staff that is not active in producing revenue.

In a service business, you might require very little office space. Basically, all you'll need is a desk, letterhead stationery, business cards, telephone, fax machine, and computer.

In a service business, you may not run into any local zoning difficulties. If you are running a consulting business out of your extra bedroom, chances are no one will know about it. If, on the other hand, you're trying to produce a "whatever" in your garage and trucks are pulling up to take it away, you will not last long in a residential neighborhood.

The tax advantages of one's own business are quite substantial. Many expenses you incur right now are legitimate business expenses once you are established, such as the space, maintenance, phone, travel, possibly automobile use, business travel, and attendance fees for special seminars and conferences.

VOLUNTEER WORK

All volunteer work is important and valuable and satisfying, whether it involves helping out in a hospital, making phone calls for the political candidate of your choice, or working with disadvantaged children.

In a relatively new development, business executives have begun volunteering their *business* skills. A fair number of senior executive men, and a growing number of women, are volunteering to help young, entrepreneurial businesses; volunteering to train disadvantaged high-school and college students; or volunteering to work with the skilled handicapped.

These same people are volunteering their services for local, state, and even federal government projects that are underfunded and in need of expertise. This is particularly satisfying work.

In addition to the obvious benefits you get to bestow, this kind of volunteer work gives you an opportunity to keep up your contacts and interact with people in your field.

....

Be sure to carefully explore your options to reduce unexpected difficulties when choosing second careers.

....

Volunteer work is an excellent first stop-off for those who face early retirement, especially involuntary early retirement. Volunteer work of any sort provides enormous psychological benefits in that you have an opportunity to help in an area you care about, frequently providing services to those less fortunate or simply those looking for a chance, and you will most probably receive sincere gratitude, something you may not have necessarily experienced often in your corporate life.

Beyond the psychological advantages, volunteer work can be an excellent way to test a new field or profession in the areas that interest you most, on your own timetable. Most charities, for example, in addition to relying heavily on volunteers, maintain a paid full-time staff as well. Those positions are usually filled by people who started as volunteers and became deeply involved with the work of the charity and in some cases simply became indispensable.

If you have the time and financial resources to coast for a while without immediately replacing your income, volunteer work can make a lot of sense, give you a psychological boost, and provide immediate work satisfaction and flexibility.

WRITE AND SPEAK PUBLICLY

It is a common complaint at corporations today that recent college graduates come to corporate life with poor writing and speaking skills. During the 1980s, technology was stressed, MBAs were fashionable, computer literacy became essential. Although this educational direction made sense for the times, it is unfortunate that it was occasionally at the expense of developing writing and speaking skills.

In our communications-oriented corporate environment, there's no place to hide. You must be able to write a letter, write a memo, write an in-depth report, write (on occasion) for your trade magazine or newspaper or organization, and be able to present the same material "on your feet." It is essential that you can address a meeting, address employees, address alumni.

44

It is worthwhile and smart for you to volunteer for any and all writing and speaking opportunities in your area of expertise prior to your retirement. While most of these assignments may be unpaid, they build a portfolio for you and they build experience. Women nearing retirement age right now tend to have been better trained in the writing and public-speaking areas than their younger colleagues. This is an advantage that you should run with.

The best way to get paid writing assignments and paid speaking assignments is for someone to spot your unpaid writing or unpaid speaking and open other opportunities to you. Once you are aggressively seeking paid writing assignments and paid speaking assignments, you will have to start with the less desirable options and work your way up to the better ones. For instance, in writing, you may find that you can generate some fees from your trade magazine or newspaper, local newspaper, magazine start-ups in your field, and research-oriented academic assignments. Becoming a book author overnight is probably not a real possibility until you have been reasonably widely published in magazines or newspapers.

On the speaking front, the least desirable assignments tend to be for trade groups, charities that offer only a modest honorarium, your alma mater, or your local political party. The next speaking level is for student groups on campuses, although these engagements pay only modest fees and, unfortunately, college campuses tend to be in out-of-the-way locations, requiring involved transportation arrangements. If you're serious about pursuing your writing and speaking, though, take whatever comes along and do your absolute best to follow up with any contacts you make through these engagements. Eventually, if you have polished your skills and know your material, these will lead to more lucrative and pleasant assignments.

Although it's difficult to make a decent living either writing or speaking, again, as part of an overall income-generating plan, speaking and writing can play an important role.

TEACH

Teaching is an attractive alternative in retirement, largely because the academic world looks for and values the main thing that the corporate world often seems to ignore or disparage, namely one's age, experience, and wisdom. In much of the corporate world, younger is thought to be better, more interesting, more lively, more salable. In academia, wisdom and knowledge and experience are the better attributes. Consequently, from a psychological standpoint, it's hard to beat teaching.

Teaching also offers the advantage of time-management flexibility. If you choose to teach, you can do it full time, part time, on a volunteer basis, for pay, during the summer, at home, abroad, in the country, in the city. This great flexibility in time management and, peripherally, in geographical location is appealing, especially to those who have spent twenty or thirty years working nine to five in a rigid hierarchy.

If you have worked, you are probably qualified to teach something. Teaching accreditation is monitored on a state-by-state basis, and you will need to check with your state education board regarding requirements for teaching lower school, middle school, high school, college, graduate school, and adult education courses. The chances are that you could probably quickly qualify for teaching below the high-school level in your state by putting in time at a state university in order to obtain the necessary credits and certification. High-school teaching might require more work, and college teaching most certainly will require advanced study and possibly even an advanced degree. Most universities, however, now offer adult education courses in addition to those at the graduate and undergraduate level. Qualifications required for teaching adult education are much less stringent and you should not overlook that possibility.

If teaching appeals to you, you should outline for yourself those subjects in which you have an interest or are qualified and then prepare to meet the requirements to teach at the level that you prefer.

Teaching even one course a week at either the high-school, college, or adult education level not only would provide income, but will open up the possibility of participating in available benefits at the institution, such as group insurance plans. This teaching experience should also open up for you new contacts, the possibility of writing in your field for publication, and opportunities to participate in related educational activities. Travel options may be there as well.

The drawback to teaching is salary and compensation. Unless you qualify to teach at the college level or beyond, you will find that teaching salaries do not compare or compete with those available in the corporate world. Nevertheless, as a stepping stone, or as part of an overall income-producing scenario that includes other activities, teaching is an excellent option in retirement.

A good example of retiring onto something is shown by an interesting couple I recently met, both in their forties, with a ten-year-old son. I met them when they pulled up in their truck to rescue my boat in a small Long Island marina, which was in the process of sinking after a two-day downpour. The entire family rather quickly pumped it out and generally rescued it from its fate. I was interested and amused to note that all three of them had on overalls sporting the name of their boatyard, which was also emblazoned on their truck. We started a conversation and I discovered that while they now lived year round in a small town on Long Island and ran the local boatyard, they had bought it, with another couple their age, just two years earlier. Both couples were from New York and had worked in computer programming. The two couples had been friends during their marriages and the birth of their children, and had spent years complaining about life in New York and speculating about what it would be like to live in a healthy environment—back to nature and all of that sort of thing.

....

An alternative lifestyle often holds great appeal for people of all ages.

....

One weekend, about two and a half years ago, while looking for a used boat, they made the acquaintance of the then-owner of their boatyard, who was seventy-five years old and for the first time in his life thinking about retiring. They told him they were thinking about retiring, too, although they were thirty years younger. They explained that they wanted to retire from the pressure and grind of their metropolitan existences, and they told him that they envied him his healthy lifestyle. Apparently about sixty days later, the four of them quit their jobs in New York and bought the boatyard. They sold their apartments, cashed in their savings, investments, and retirement plans, pooled their money, and purchased the boatyard.

The couple I spoke to said that it had dramatically changed their lives, primarily for the best. They loved what they were doing and felt physically and mentally healthier. They also pointed out that they were living on about 40 percent of the income they had grown accustomed to in New York City and that they expected it to be ten years before they could approximate the standard of living they had had there when, in each case, the couple's joint income was approximately $100,000. They were also quick to point out that their workdays were now in fact longer than the workdays they'd put in in their computer programming jobs— approximately nine to ten hours each. It's a very different lifestyle now, however, and they certainly have an equity position. Two years into this new life, they have just begun to do the financial planning for their next retirement. They are currently aiming for age seventy, apparently inspired by the former boatyard owner.

Part Two

Planning Successfully for Retirement

Chapter 6

Guiding Your Career Toward Retirement

~~~~~~

*Questions Are Intensifying About Insurance
Safety Net*

*The faltering economy is casting a shadow over virtually
all aspects of American life, and insurance is no exception. Many insurance companies have invested heavily in
real estate or junk bonds whose market value has declined sharply, making them more vulnerable to in-
solvency.*

*Will state-guaranteed funds be adequate enough to
avert a crisis?*

—THE NEW YORK TIMES, NOVEMBER 3, 1990

From the very beginning of your career, you must
always be mindful that at the same time you are working
toward and achieving your present-day goals, you are con-
sciously, or unconsciously, guiding your career toward your
own retirement. Every year you will be faced with choices
that appear on the surface to relate only to the present but
have a dramatic effect long range.

Such choices include which field of endeavor you
choose, which corporation (will it be large or small?) you
decide to work for, and which employee benefits you select,
including the all-important health benefits. You will also

53

have choices relating to development of skills. It can be difficult to pass up an opportunity to proceed in a direction that makes sense today even if it provides little in the way of skills that will be useful to you in your fifties and sixties.

At all times you must prepare yourself for change. Few people like change and certainly fewer still ever seek it out, but it is frequently thrust upon you during your career. It's a good idea to start thinking about a second source of income early in your career, when you don't actually need it.

In the end, the important thing is being able to rid yourself of the notion that your adult life will consist of working twenty-five or thirty years so that you can have twenty-five or thirty years of leisure. Rather, you need to understand that your career, income-generating activities, and productive life simply take new turns and new directions after fifty, after sixty, after seventy, even after eighty.

···

Utilize employment opportunities with future benefits in mind.

···

This book proceeds on the premise that you will be retired, voluntarily or involuntarily, at approximately age sixty-two. Let's assume your life span is approximately eighty-two years. The prudent thing to do is to plan to finance your own retirement. If you are fortunate enough to benefit from a husband's retirement planning, so much the better. But in a volatile workplace where funding for pensions and health care is under attack and, in some cases, drying up, a husband's benefits could, in fact, be a minor part of your retirement income. Also, there is the prospect that you could have a spouse who becomes dependent on your retirement income. Which all brings us back to the premise that seems to make sense, namely that you plan to finance your retirement yourself. Here, then, are the guidelines you must follow.

54

CONSIDER HEALTH BENEFITS

Remember as you pursue your career goals that you have two career objectives: first, to satisfy all of your needs and requirements during the time you are employed, and second, to do the same for the period in which you are likely to be retired. They could each be approximately the same number of years.

With this in mind, as you move to the second and third tiers of your career, keep sight of the big picture. Of course you want to be doing something stimulating and satisfying in your field, but you also want decent benefits, those that meet your current needs, as well as those that will serve you long term.

It is also during these second and third tiers in your career that there could be a drastic increase in your stress level and a vulnerability to certain illnesses and injuries. Although it's hard to document such an occurrence, there appears to be substantial evidence that downward mobility of any sort and career traumas do lead to certain mental and physical difficulties. These could all come at the very same time that you either totally lose your health benefits or find yourself with reduced benefits that don't include any kind of preventative care or psychiatric/psychological therapy.

Because of all of the above, it's wise to explore health options while you are comfortably employed and enjoying your employee-related benefits.

OBTAIN ADDITIONAL SKILLS

You also want to be certain that you're being trained for more than what you are currently doing, so that if you need to make a move, either into an entirely new field or to a new physical location, you will be equipped to handle it.

The most readily transferable skill is sales experience. Whatever your field of endeavor, if you can spend a couple of years in sales and marketing, you will find that that one item on your résumé will make you employable in a wide variety of fields. You may say no, you're the creative type, or the technical type or whatever. Nevertheless, you give yourself an enormous boost and something of a safety net if you spend some time in sales. Anyone can sell—it simply comes easier to certain types than others.

It's also very useful to know how to position and market your product. If you can do it for your product, chances are you can do it for another, possibly even unrelated, product.

As more and more of American industry falls into the hands of foreign ownership, you should keep in mind that foreigners look for very specific, measurable experience in hiring new employees. You are best off if you have had some sales and marketing experience, supervised a sizable number of people, and had some bottom-line responsibility. All of that, combined with having worked closely with the person in charge, can make you a very desirable job candidate.

Consequently, when you make your second and/or third corporate move, make a checklist in advance of those items that will enhance your résumé and your marketability down the line. Try to achieve as many of these objectives as possible with any move, along with, of course, substantial increases in salaries, bonuses, sales incentives, and benefits.

CONSIDER TYPES OF CORPORATIONS

In America, the traditional, old-time, big corporations were and are frequently paternalistic. A family atmosphere is sought. Authority emanates from the top. The employee joins the company "for life." The corporation knows best, about the needs of the company, the direction of individual employee careers, even about major social issues. In exchange for guidance, protection, and a place to settle in, the employee is expected not to cause any trouble, not to job-hunt, and not to embarrass the company. Loyalty and hard work are valued.

A paternalistic corporation can provide a warm and wonderful atmosphere in which to work. It's easy to get lulled into the feeling that this will go on forever, that you will be taken care of, that you will be rewarded regularly.

What happens, however, if the owner of this paternalistic corporation dies, retires, sells the company, or goes out of business?

First of all, you may get a nasty surprise. It could be that during your years at the paternalistic corporation, you may not have been motivated to keep up with what's happened in your field. You may not know how marketable you are. For instance, you may not have a realistic fix on the sort of job your qualifications will earn you on the outside, the sort of salary you might expect, and the most current information regarding your peers and competitors at other companies in your field.

It is not unusual for paternalistic companies to compensate you beyond the limits of your basic salary and benefits. When you try to duplicate coverage of these expenses on your own, it can be extremely difficult. If you are accustomed to having nearly all of your health needs covered, and having a comfortable expense account (for travel, dining, theater, sports events, work-related supplies such as magazine subscriptions, books, etc.), you will probably find it costly to match this.

The next company for which you are likely to work, which could be smaller if you stay in your same field, might also not be so conveniently located and you could find yourself commuting longer and spending more money for this.

In a smaller company, it is likely that you will also have

the burden of having to wear more professional hats than you may have worn in the past. Support services that are available in a large company, such as a mail room, photocopying department, personnel, corporate travel agents, company cars, a research department, may all be missing from your new lineup.

CONSIDER CHANGING TRENDS

With our soft economy and large, previously generous corporations trimming fat, downsizing, and eliminating benefits, you will likely find a number of scenarios changing.

One such troublesome trend is that corporations are making an aggressive effort to replace full-time employees, who may be entitled to health benefits, pensions, profit sharing, expense accounts, and company cars, with part-time and free-lance people, who turn out pretty much the same work on a flat fee or hourly basis, thereby eliminating in many cases up to 40 percent of the cost for the corporation. If you become one of these free-lance contributors, you will immediately note that these previously covered expenses become your responsibility. On the other hand, smaller companies may offer greater autonomy, the possibility of some equity, more flexible hours, and less rigid requirements for advancement.

PLANNING FROM DAY ONE: A BEST-CASE SCENARIO

If you are just starting out, perhaps in your early to middle twenties and newly graduated from college, graduate school, law school, or medical school, you will find yourself in an extremely advantageous position if you consider retirement planning from day one. Although retirement may appear to be forty years away, there could be interruptions for marriage, childbirth, child rearing, illness (your own, your spouse's, your aging parents'), job loss, and other hard-to-predict factors.

....

It is not unwise to view your entire work experience in light of the retirement opportunities it has to offer.

....

You're just starting out, your mind is on your career. You're looking for fame, fortune, glory, or at least a little excitement. Something interesting. You're probably focusing on salary. Starting salaries are low everywhere, but especially so in certain fields. Nevertheless, stick with the field that you're interested in and try to find a first job that offers a decent salary, experience in a healthy, progressive, creative company, and at least an outside chance to build your career as part of their operation.

When you think of what you'll be paid, consider both the bottom-line salary and the kinds of benefits the company offers. You are likely to encounter one of two setups.

First, many traditional old-line companies offer health insurance benefits (these generally have at least a hundred-dollar annual deductible, and reimburse you for perhaps 80 percent of your medical expenses, not including dental work, eye exams, plastic surgery, or psychological care). In addition to basic health coverage, you may get life insurance, equal to perhaps your annual salary. And you may be offered the opportunity to start investing in a pension fund. Many large companies still offer pension funds in which your contribution is matched by a contribution from the company. Smaller companies, without their own funded pension program, may offer a 401-K plan, which is an opportunity for you to set aside certain funds, tax free, and make withdrawals in your retirement of the amount you put in, plus the interest earned and any matching funds your employer made. Taxes are due when you start making withdrawals, but presumably you will be in a lower tax bracket then.

A very few companies offer disability insurance as well, but it is generally reserved for those at the vice presidential level or above. If you have any opportunity to sign on for it, by all means do.

A second possible benefits scenario is one in which you are offered a "cafeteria benefit program." Such a program offers you a chance to pick and choose from various benefits, which can include life insurance, health insurance, extra vacation pay, day care for small children, and time off to care for dependent parents. When you are starting out, especially if you're single, it's tempting to skip the life insurance and health insurance and take the extra vacation. This is a big mistake. You should *always* cover your health insurance needs before considering any other kinds of benefits. Second to health insurance should be a chance to invest in some kind of pension or retirement plan. It's a form of forced savings, and if you start out setting aside something for the retirement phase of your life, you will get in the habit of doing so and the money will be there when you need it.

When you're starting your career, you're focused on your salary and benefits, but don't forget your position. I don't mean title, I mean position. In order to protect your future earnings, it works best if you can start in a position where you'll learn a lot, be exposed to a variety of situations, and, if possible, work for someone with decision-making power—the higher up the ladder, the better. The best kind of training you can get in a starting position is a chance to watch the action, to see how the critical decisions in your company are made and who makes them.

A generation or two ago, a starting employee could hope to make her entire career at one or perhaps two companies. The plan would be to learn, contribute, and receive salary increases, promotions, and opportunities based on merit. Unfortunately, though, we now live in a very unstable corporate environment, one in which downsizing, mergers, and more recently bankruptcies have become common. Such activity inevitably involves significant layoffs, at all levels.

While company loyalty and identity are still to be admired, it's wise to keep your options open, from the very beginning. Make sure that you are on the cutting edge of your field. Constantly upgrade your technical skills; most important, become computer literate if you aren't already.

Be realistic about what your marketable skills really are, and give thought to how readily transferable they are to another field if such a transfer becomes necessary.

If your company offers opportunities to fund additional formal education for you, by all means take advantage of it.

Simultaneously with orienting yourself in your first career position, start a lifetime savings habit. Take at least 5 percent of your gross pay every payday and put it in either a savings account or money market fund, so that it is liquid. Keep saving until you have amassed an amount equal to three or, even better, six months of basic expenses (rent or mortgage, taxes, insurance, car, food). Once you have established this emergency fund, you can begin investing your savings in a wider variety of ways, such as in low-risk mutual funds.

As you are starting out, don't get into debt, which can become a lifelong difficulty. Any debt you incur at this point should be small and manageable, the result of perhaps one or two major purchases for your home charged on a major credit card. Get into the habit of making the monthly payments right away. Don't use credit cards for luxuries and other items that are not necessary.

One credit card, paid off on time, helps to build your credit rating. Opening a bank account and borrowing a small sum for an important purchase, also paid off on time, will benefit your credit rating as well.

No matter how many years you think you will continue to work at this time, chances are you will work longer than that, and you absolutely will need your own good credit rating.

MID-CAREER PLANNING

By your mid-thirties or early forties, you may have achieved a position of department or division head, or vice president. Your benefits may be quite acceptable, in fact generous. Nevertheless, it's time to think about the possibility of having an equity position in something.

....

Equity is an important part of retirement strategy.

....

Review your skills and experience and see if there isn't an opportunity for you to start a small business in your own name, perhaps in consulting, writing, teaching, or speaking. Don't look initially to this business to replace your current salary. View it as a supplement. View it as part of your safety net for the future.

Even though your current employment position might seem stable, your corporation is healthy, and you may be well known in your field, still, the odds are that sometime in the near future you could confront a corporate merger or takeover, serious downsizing, or the prospect of being urged to retire early. And, of course, there's always the nasty prospect of simply being fired.

Honestly assess your contribution to the bottom line of

your company. Could someone, albeit with less experience, be hired to replace you for less money? Are you working in a support department, such as advertising, promotion, even personnel, where early corporate cuts tend to start?

Remember, even if your position is stable, the best retirements are not financed with one big check a month. Just like it's good to spread the risk in investments, it's good to spread the source of retirement income.

Perhaps you will be in demand at your current corporation and asked to stay on until at least sixty-five, or even seventy, if you're one of the lucky few. And you may be looking forward to collecting Social Security and reaping the benefits of your long-term savings and investments. Regardless, it will be very comforting if there is also a monthly check from your outside consulting, a quarterly royalty check from one or more books that you have produced, and an occasional speaking fee. Also remember that all of these outside activities broaden your professional base.

Any thoughts of entrepreneurship and owning your own business should really be "on the side" at this point. There is no need to incur overhead and staff salaries or, more importantly, to risk your current paycheck, benefits, and access to an office and office services.

After a year or so of assessing the possibilities of starting your own business, and perhaps several months of successfully running a business on the side, it might be time to entertain the possibility of stepping out on your own at fifty or, say, fifty-five.

Discreetly inquire as to your company's policies on retirement, early retirement, part-time work, benefits, pensions, and profit sharing. If there are any rumblings at this point that your company is looking to cut costs by laying off expensive senior employees in favor of less expensive, even part-time, cheaper employees, by all means speed up your efforts.

Simultaneously, it's always wise to try to make yourself

indispensable at your company while you are laying your master plan.

At this point you should check in with your attorney and accountant regarding their feelings on the options open to you: remaining where you are full time, accepting an early-retirement package, forming your own business.

All of these steps are easier to take from your comfortable corporate position. Just as it's simpler to borrow money from a bank when you don't need it, it is simpler to get your own consulting or service business going when you don't need to rely on it for your total livelihood.

At this time it's also a good idea to pull out your file of letters from people who have approached you in the past regarding employment. Perhaps you have several in there from companies you passed on at the time because you didn't wish to relocate. As you enter your fifties, they could make perfect consulting clients.

Owning your own business has many advantages, not the least of which is the favorable tax treatment of expenses incurred for your business location, phone, supplies, travel, and staff. In many cases these may be expenses you're incurring now, on your own, and have never been able to deduct.

If you own your own business, no matter how small the operation, you also have an employment base, basically forever. Unless you take in partners or have outside investors, both of whom would have a say in the matter, you can run the business until you're ninety-five if you want to.

....

Review early-retirement packages carefully.

....

Let's assume here a fairly common scenario. You're on good terms with your employer. You're fairly high up in the organization and you're doing a good job. You are approached, in a friendly and supportive way, to consider early retirement. On the surface at least, the package looks very appealing: a lump-sum payment up front, at least a partial pension, and at least partial continuing health benefits. You need to immediately take several steps.

First, consult with your attorney regarding the legality of the offer and what its components really mean.

Second, on your own or with your accountant, figure out the real dollar value of what they are offering you versus what you would have if you stayed.

Third, try to read the political climate. If you sense they are being nice now but, if you don't take the package, plan to force you out early or fire you, go back to them with a counteroffer—perhaps better terms of the lump sum, the piece of the pension, and the piece of the health benefits.

On top of that, it is also important to seek a five-year consulting arrangement, even for a modest sum, whereby you continue to provide a service similar to that which you now provide full time. Such an arrangement has many advantages for you. First, you're still associated with your corporation. Second, you can use your corporation as a business reference in seeking other consulting clients. Third, you'll have at least occasional use of an office and office support services.

Perhaps the handwriting is on the wall and this is the best offer you are going to get. If you can combine it with a consulting arrangement, though, it launches you in the best possible way in your own business and toward other potentially lucrative and prestigious clients.

LOSING YOUR CAREER: A WORST-CASE SCENARIO

Now let's assume the worst-case scenario. You are summarily fired. You are told that the company can't afford you

anymore and your position or department has been eliminated. You get some severance pay (generally one week's
pay for every year you've been with the company). You get
the opportunity (which they have to give you legally anyway) to convert your health insurance over to your own
policy, which you will eventually have to pay yourself. You
get, if you were part of a pension plan to start with, your
pension funds as a lump sum with the opportunity to roll the
money over into an IRA to avoid immediate taxation.

This experience can be psychologically devastating, de-
pressing, humiliating, embarrassing. You will feel all of
these things. You will also feel vulnerable, your self-esteem
will drop to an all-time low, and fear and anxiety will set in.
How are you going to pay your bills? Will you ever find
another job? What did you do wrong?

These feelings will pass. Most likely, they will be replaced by enormous anger, even rage. If you're fortunate,
this will channel itself into activity. First of all, remember you
cannot be fired for age alone. That is ageism. It is against the
law. Every day major lawsuits are filed and won on this
basis. Chances are, however, that even if that's the real
reason you are being fired, your corporation will have been
smart enough to have positioned it in another way.

Your first call should be to your attorney, who should
set up a meeting with your former employer to investigate
what has happened. What was the reason for your firing.
Was it properly handled? Can any of the items promised to
you be improved upon? Will the company pay for outplacement services for you?

Outplacement companies are not employment agen-
cies. They don't have a ready list of available jobs. Rather,
they help you adjust to your new, unemployed situation.
They provide counseling and group discussion. They help
you prepare résumés and letters. They put you in touch with
human resources departments at corporations where your

skills might best be used. Finally, they offer financial-planning assistance to get you through what can be a long, dry period with no income other than your severance pay or unemployment compensation. The rule of thumb is that it takes up to one week of job hunting for every thousand dollars you earn. You can quickly see that if you are making more than $50,000 a year, you could be out of work, or at least out of full-time work, for a year or more.

In the midst of all of this trauma, however, there are forces working in your favor. First of all, America faces an ever-increasing shortage of experienced, technically trained workers. If you have stayed on top of your industry in all ways, including technologically, you might be pleasantly surprised at the openings available to you. While they are most likely to be in newer, smaller companies, a switch from a large corporation to a smaller, more entrepreneurial firm can be an invigorating experience. You might find yourself the resident expert in your area, much sought out by younger, less experienced staff.

These smaller, newer firms are also likely to be interested in you on a part-time or consulting basis, as well. If you're laying your plans for ten or more years, you might welcome the opportunity to work two or three days a week at your former profession, while freeing up time to write, speak, or teach.

Again, I want to emphasize that if you can sell, speak well, and write well, you will find your skills amazingly, readily transferable.

Chapter 7

Retirement and Your Own Business

❧❧❧

Women currently own approximately one-third of all small businesses in the United States. The number of small businesses started by women is growing at four times the rate of those started by men. There are many explanations for this.

First, women in their forties, fifties, and sixties who are currently in the workforce frequently experience what's known as the "glass ceiling." The glass ceiling is either real or perceived, but its effect is the same. Women reach a certain point in the corporation and mysteriously they go no further. The very top jobs are not open to them. Many of these women are highly qualified, and it's out of the frustration of being stalled at a certain point in the corporate hierarchy that they look to the possibility of starting their own businesses.

Another large group of women find themselves retired, either voluntarily or involuntarily, and do not possess the funds to maintain their lifestyle.

Yet another group was living life in retirement with their spouse, and either the spouse died or the spouse's funding (investments, pension funds, his own business) ceased to provide the necessary funds.

....

If you have entrepreneurial skills, owning a business can be rewarding.

....

Starting and owning a business can take many forms: full time, part time, alone, with others, with little or no investment, with a substantial investment.

If starting and owning your own business looks like an appealing idea for your retirement, you need to answer the first questions of any entrepreneur:

1. How would you define the business you wish to start?

2. Is this business in an area or field that you know something about, or, ideally, a lot about?

3. Is it a business you can operate yourself, or will you need the input of partners or employees?

4. Is there anyone doing what you want to do, and if so, can you do it better, more efficiently, or more profitably?

5. Is your business going to provide a service or produce a product? The chances are great that it will provide a service, since product businesses require production, inventories, manufacturing, and distribution.

Probably the most important question you can ask yourself, though, is: Are you an entrepreneurial woman? If you want to be an entrepreneur, it's helpful if you possess the classic entrepreneurial personality. Are you independent? Organized? A self-starter? Energetic? Optimistic? Gregarious? Charismatic?

Do you handle people well, whether they work for you or with you or you work for them? Are you focused? Do you tend to go right to the core of the matter? Are you single-minded? Are you healthy? Are you creative?

The more yeses you are able to give to those questions, the more naturally you will fit the role of the entrepreneur. No one possesses all of these qualities, but if you are quite the reverse type, not only will your business probably either not get off the ground or fail, but you'll be unhappy. If you like lots of company and human interaction, work best when supervised, tend to have a rather pessimistic view of things, have difficulty getting along with people, have a dependent nature, and hate risk, you should absolutely not pursue an entrepreneurial venture. Instead, you belong in a group or partnership of some sort where strong direction is provided and your exposure to risk and anxiety are limited.

Let's assume, however, that you are generally an entrepreneurial type, you are skilled and experienced through corporate life, and you like risk. You have retired early and find that your combined Social Security, pension (if available), and profit sharing will not cover your expenses. Perhaps even more important, you have no desire to spend the next thirty years in the hot pursuit of leisure. You thrive on challenges, excitement, success. You want to stay in the mainstream and make a contribution. You are possibly even addicted to your field of interest.

Unless money is no object, you will want to start your service business either out of your home, or even on the side while you are fully employed. (If at all possible, this will be with the approval of your employer, who is going to be your first client.)

Women starting their own businesses, like men, tend to form a company that either continues to do what they were doing for someone else, or pursues what was once a hobby, or provides an unrelated service or product for which the entrepreneur has seen a longtime need.

If you decide to work at home, perhaps out of an extra bedroom, converted garage, basement, or attic, be certain there are no zoning restrictions against your activity. Also check to see if there are local licenses or permits required— for instance, if you are planning a day-care center for children, or senior citizens, in your converted basement. Along these lines, if you are planning to manufacture or even serve food as part of your activity at home, you will want to check with the health department.

FEASIBILITY STUDY

Your first step in starting a business should be to define your business and to establish in writing that it is viable as a profitable enterprise. You will need to establish the following:

- Your market
- How you are going to reach your market
- The cost of reaching your market
- Any competition
- How you differ from the competition
- Start-up capital required (phone, fax, office supplies, secretarial assistance, services of your accountant, attorney, and banker)

- Licenses, permits, certification required
- Number of employees required—full time or free-lance (calculate cost of salaries and benefits)
- Cost of producing and distributing your service

PROJECTION OF CASH FLOW FOR THE FIRST YEAR

You need to prepare a rough projection of your cash flow for the first year. This is all income less all expenses, including your cash outlay up front. Do this on a monthly basis, remembering always that while everyone bills on time, not everyone pays on time. Figure out the time required. Are you going to be doing this full time or part time?

Once you have worked out all of your assumptions, it would make sense to review your assessment of your feasability with your attorney and possibly your accountant and banker. If the outside expert help you seek is from people who have been involved in previous business start-ups, you will save yourself a lot of time and nasty surprises.

THE BUSINESS PLAN

If you and your outside advisers have established that your business is feasible, that there's a market for it, that you can provide the service and are likely to show a profit, then the next step is developing a business plan.

....

A business plan is an essential investment.

....

The purpose of a business plan is to establish what you need in terms of time, money, staff, and supplies in order to provide your service and collect the fees due you for it. If your business is going to require an up-front investment of your funds or someone else's, the business plan needs to show when the business will "turn"—that is, when it will start showing positive cash flow. Positive cash flow is not profit, it simply means you are taking in enough money each month to pay your bills, hopefully with a little left over.

A profit is determined at the end of the year when you take all income less all expenses, less payments due plus receivables.

Your business plan also needs to project the likelihood that you have developed a potentially ongoing business. Your business needs to be able to survive year after year and deal with competition, changes in the economy, changes in the tax law, and changes in the demographic makeup of your market.

Your business plan needs to include the following:

- Definition of your business

- Staff required

- Cash outlay up front, including office supplies, possibly office space, insurance, review by outside experts, lease or purchase of equipment such as computer, fax, copier

- Estimate of the amount of business you will do, by month, for one year

- Number of clients and the gross income you are likely to generate from each of them

- All expenses required to provide service for one-year period

- Any cost of borrowing money
- Cost of any certification, licenses, permits

Whatever your business, you will most certainly be laying out money for at least the first three to six months, rather than taking it in. You must be realistic about your cash flow and be conservative in estimating likely income, as well as the time span required to collect it.

Your feasibility study and business plan are basically for you and any partners you intend to bring in at the start of your business.

As a new business owner, you should primarily expect to sell—yourself, as well as your services—to clients, suppliers, staff, and potential investors. The new business owner must feel a real excitement and dedication to her business. If she does, it is more likely to thrive.

The new business owner needs to be visible, as visible as anyone in the corporate world. This means seeking out press interviews (possibly also radio and TV) and speaking engagements (whether paid or not). The entrepreneur should strive to be a major presence in her field. If she already has been one at her corporation, she should keep up her involvement on all fronts.

Special Considerations in Retirement Planning:

Children, Aging Parents, Marital Status

~~~~~

ACTION IN THE CONGRESS

On January 31, 1991, Representative William J. Hughes from New Jersey, the Chairman of the Sub-Committee on Retirement Income and Employment of the House Select Committee on Aging, sent the following letter:

I will shortly be introducing the "The Social Security Caregivers Act of 1991" to recognize the millions of caregivers across America who care for our children and the elderly. Despite contributing thousands, if not millions, of dollars to the Social Security program in taxes, many of the 53 million working women will reach retirement or face widowhood with diminished incomes because the years they spent caregiving significantly decreased their Social Security benefit.

While women often assume the majority of caregiving responsibilities, spending on average 11½ years out of the work force caring for children or elderly parents, compared to 1.3 years for men, the Social Security program does not recognize those years. Rather, it penalizes them by averaging a zero into their benefit computation, thereby reducing their monthly benefits. Social Security benefits are based on a thirty-five-year work life, even though most women will never accumulate thirty-five years of work history due to their caregiving responsibilities. Women's Social Security benefits lag behind men's, and the gap is not closing. The average Social Security benefit for men is $627 and for women $458 a month.

"The Social Security Caregivers Act of 1991" will allow any worker, male or female, to drop out up to five of years of either zero or very low earnings from their benefit calculation, if that year is devoted to caregiving. I strongly believe this bill takes an important first step towards addressing some of the inequities and inadequacies of the Social Security program.

We can all agree that Social Security has done an admirable job at keeping millions of elderly and disabled Americans out of poverty. It has enabled millions of Americans to live independently and with dignity in their retirement years. It is now time to make some changes to adapt to America's working family of the 1990s. Demographics indicate that more and more women and men will be called upon to serve as their families' caregiver. In fact, it has been estimated that the need for caregivers will almost triple over the next four decades. Unless a change is made, the Social Security Administration will continue to average zeroes into millions of workers' benefits because the program assumes a worker will be in the paid labor force for thirty-five years.

CHILDREN

Perhaps you've read this far in the book and you say, "Well, this is all well and good, but I'm a wife and mother and am not able to orchestrate my life this flawlessly."

Well, you're in the majority. Most women marry at some point and most of those women have children. This is the main reason women enter the workforce late, sometimes ten years later than men, and/or interrupt their careers after perhaps a five- or ten-year start.

Because the standard employment scenario that I painted earlier in the book is, in fact, enjoyed mainly by men and women with no children, if you do have children, you must recognize the impact they will have on your retirement planning and be inventive about customizing your own plan.

I'm a mother and my daughter is my first priority. Even so, I know that one day I will wish to retire and that I'll have to fund my retirement. I have tried to customize my career and business experience in a way so that she can remain my top priority while at the same time planning responsibly for later years of my employment and my retirement.

....

The special concerns of retiring women are often overlooked or ignored.

....

In my opinion, women with children cannot afford to totally stop their careers in midstream or keep from starting them until they are perhaps in their thirties. The main reason is that this will give you fewer years of a top salary, fewer years in which to make contacts, fewer years in which to establish the credentials necessary to switch fields if necessary or start your own business, fewer years to pay into a pension fund.

A better scenario is one in which you get your career started early, just like the men, and if it becomes necessary to interrupt it, you make sure the interruption is not full time. In other words, if you have started a career in health, publishing, finance, law, or any other profession, don't flee to the suburbs, physically or mentally, 100 percent, upon the birth of your first child. Even if you decide to stay home part time or full time, for several months or several years, keep all of your contacts open and active. If you've spent five or ten years with a corporation, approach them and try to lay a plan in which you work part time at the office or at home.

With the advent of the fax machine and the computer, along with the telephone and overnight-mail services, you can certainly continue to function for your company, even at a distance.

Or you might persuade your employer to pair you with another new mother eager to work part time and allow the two or three of you to fulfill the job requirements of one person and split the salary accordingly.

Your objective during this time is not primarily financial. The extra money is sure to be useful with the birth of a child, but more importantly, you stay in the mainstream, keep your contacts open, continue to be involved with and important to your company, and maintain your career track.

If you can combine motherhood with continued activity at the office, and perhaps work on an advanced degree, such as an MBA, you will succeed in having it both ways. You'll have the joy of relatively full-time motherhood with the continued intellectual stimulation of your career, and possibly even completion of a few courses toward an advanced degree, which will catapult you ahead in your career when you return full time.

Women—even those who held the most promise in the early years of their careers—who totally disassociate themselves from their field for two or three or five or more years find it extremely difficult to reenter.

First of all, everyone will have forgotten what a hotshot you were or the quality of your contribution. Second, a whole new group of young women will have entered the company, presumably with credentials at least as good as yours. Third, every field advances technologically at a rapid pace, and unless you've kept informed about this important area, chances are you won't even be able to do the job you left five years ago.

My own experience with new motherhood was full of surprises but worked relatively well for the baby, my employer, and myself. Although I took only one month of full maternity leave, I was fortunate in that I lived only eight blocks from my office. I employed a full-time baby nurse, and my employer, knowing that I wanted to spend a great deal of time with the baby, accepted the fact that I came in late and left early every day, for almost two years. On top of that, I went home every day for lunch—usually for about two and a half hours. I was able to work this out because I used those lunch periods not only to be with the baby but also to orchestrate business lunches. These went amazingly well at my apartment (with the help of a cook/housekeeper). Since I worked in publishing at the time, much of the work I did involved reading, writing, and speaking into my dictaphone. I was able to do all of this while the baby slept. I always felt as though I was a full-time mother, and in fact the baby nurse would tell me that the baby was always asleep the whole time I was at the office, anyway. While this situation wasn't perfect, it gave me the time that both the baby and I needed, and it also gave my employer the work he needed to have done.

While I certainly wasn't promoted during those two years, I did manage to run a department of more than forty people, manage a multimillion-dollar budget, and perform at a high level.

Once my daughter had passed her second birthday and was in nursery school, I started putting in longer hours at the office, but I also instituted a new business travel rule: I *never*, and I do mean *never*, went on any business travel without my daughter. First of all, at this point in my career, I had cut my business travel way back, from a high of more than ten weeks a year to about four weeks. Because I could, I scheduled whatever travel I had during her school vacation and took her with me, frequently with the nanny as well. This was an added expense to me, but it made her happy and it made me happy for us to be together. My daughter is now twelve and I still don't travel without her.

I also happen to be in favor of children frequently visiting the office. Not everyone feels this way, but I find it to be healthy for children to see how their mothers spend the bulk of the day.

....

It is vital to remain visible in your career, even during absences.

....

Finally, there is the issue of corporate-funded day care. There has been a flurry of news lately regarding major corporations that have built on-site day care because they are very eager to hold on to their valued female employees and have recognized that child care is extremely expensive and hard to find. Not everyone wants to leave their child in a day-care center, but those with reservations feel better about it when the center is on the same premises as their job. In such arrangements, the mother can visit with her child several times a day, including at feeding time.

While it may be possible to cleverly arrange the logistics for raising one child, the complications of two or more children are truly formidable. Unless the government, in coordination with employers, assists women with several children in the maintenance of their careers, everyone will suffer. The woman will pay the financial price further down the line. The company will lose valued employees. The husband, who may later come to rely on his wife financially, will be worse off as well.

This whole issue is the subject of seemingly endless political debate. Regardless of the general outcome, women still have to work out the details of their own arrangements, with their own husbands and families. That process goes more smoothly if everyone is properly informed about the connection between the progress of a woman's career and her later financial vulnerability or stability, as well as the vulnerability or stability of those dependent on her—children, spouse, or aging parents.

AGING PARENTS

Women have always assumed the burden of aging parents. Several generations ago, when the man worked outside the home and the woman ran the household and raised the children, this was part of the natural order. If a parent became ill or was left alone, the parent moved in with the daughter.

Several generations ago, aging parents might have had a life expectancy of, say, the late sixties or early seventies. We now live in a very different world. First of all, the fastest-growing segment of the population is the group over fifty, and of those, large numbers are reaching their eighties and even nineties. A recent article on retirement trends in *The Wall Street Journal* suggested that people facing retirement now look to a life expectancy of ninety. The difficulty is that many of those years will be spent in ill health.

While one's parents might continue the tradition of retiring in their late fifties or early sixties, chances are they could then live an additional twenty or thirty years. As their money runs out and their ability to care for themselves diminishes, the burden most usually falls on the daughter, or even the daughter-in-law. Most of these aging parents are fiercely independent and want very much to live on their own, but are ultimately unable to.

There are several categories of care required by aging parents. The first and easiest is when the parent lives nearby, is in good health, and is socially independent, but requires some assistance in grocery shopping, running errands, cooking, and transportation to medical and social appointments. While this doesn't sound like much, it can take whoever's performing the services easily ten hours a week.

If the parent falls into the second category—housebound and partially disabled—the number of hours involved can easily double or triple.

Then there is the category of parents who can no longer take care of themselves, but who do not require hospitalization. These are candidates for senior centers associated with medical facilities, or even nursing homes. Both prospects can be psychologically and financially terrifying to both the aging parent and the daughter on whom the burden falls. Faced with this kind of scenario, many women simply move their ill and dependent parents into their own homes. Such a move can require the very nearly full-time assistance of the daughter, or hiring someone full time to carry out most of the tasks.

A new and interesting alternative comes from a handful of major corporations that now offer a form of day care for healthy senior citizens. These companies mainly provide social and physical activities as well as a meal. Such an arrangement can be the difference between a woman being able to keep her job or having to give it up to care for the aging parent. Many women earning $30,000, $50,000, or $100,000 a year, when faced with the prospect of an annual nursing home bill of perhaps $30,000 in after-tax money, will opt to quit their job and stay home with the parent instead. This is a greater sacrifice even than it appears on the surface. A woman who relinquishes her job in mid-career loses not only her salary but also her seniority, her contacts, and possibly full participation in important benefits such as health insurance, profit sharing, and pensions.

Choices in this area can be painful and agonizing, and many women treat the logistics in a fashion similar to that which I noted earlier in the book, when discussing motherhood.

Women absolutely must protect themselves in terms of their long-term employment, as well as retirement, and the option of walking away from their career in the face of the needs of an aging parent or parents has to be considered with all of its ramifications.

Research has shown for quite some time that the top benefit priority of working women is some form of help with child care, and more recently the second most commonly cited need is assistance in some form for the care of aging parents.

While there is a natural human resistance to thinking about and planning ahead for unpleasant likelihoods, such as one's aging parents becoming dependent, it is a situation prevalent enough now to require attention. Women need to weigh carefully choices of benefits in a cafeteria-style plan— or even choices between companies, where care for dependent children and aging parents is offered versus those where it is not.

MARITAL STATUS

It is best, safest, and most sensible to plan to finance your own retirement. But even if you do, you could, perhaps, surprisingly to you, end up financing that of your husband or even your former husband.

If you were married at one time but aren't any longer, you will be financing your own retirement. If you were married for more than ten years, you are entitled to some payment from your husband's Social Security, and possibly pension fund, *but* it's unlikely to be a significant component in your overall retirement fund.

If you are currently married and contemplating divorce, find a matrimonial attorney who can handle the complexities of seeking your share of your husband's property, pension, profit sharing, Social Security, and future earning power. Quickie divorces, and especially those in which the woman is not properly represented, commonly shortchange the wife. Alimony is practically a thing of the past, and even when it is decreed, enforcing it can be difficult and, in many cases, cost you more money than the amount you end up recovering. Unfortunately, this goes for child support as well.

....

Preparing for the unexpected is sensible and smart, especially during retirement.

....

Any divorce settlement that you sign should take into account your years as a homemaker, possibly your years contributing to your husband's education and professional advancement, the structure of his pension plan, and/or the structure of his medical practice or legal or accounting partnership. If your husband owns his own business and you have participated in it in *any* way, you are most probably entitled to a share in the income generated from it and in the proceeds from any sale.

The flip side of this, unfortunately, is that at the very time that livable alimony and child support are disappearing, men are, with increasing frequency, suing their former wives for a share in *their* pensions, *their* professional partnerships, and, most painfully, the businesses that they have started in their own names.

If you formed your own business while married to your former husband, you can expect him to go after a piece of it. Whether or not he'll succeed depends largely on whether he can document any kind of contribution, be it financial or consulting or day-to-day participation.

Additionally, if your former husband is older than you

are—especially if he's much older—he may claim that he is unable to support himself or take care of his medical expenses, and he may in fact sue you for alimony or some kind of maintenance/support.

It certainly is disheartening to think that the very business that you might have started to finance your escape from a bad marriage could in fact be vulnerable to claims from your former husband, but that's just what happens in some cases.

If you suspect any such thing is likely to occur, you should discuss it honestly with your attorney and accountant and attempt to structure your business from the very start in such a way that your husband will have no grounds for seeking a related financial settlement.

If you are single and employed, with a nice pension and profit-sharing arrangement, and possibly even an equity position in one or more companies, you may feel invulnerable to the scenario painted above.

Unfortunately, it is not necessarily that simple. If you are living with someone and have been living with him for a fair amount of time during which you've shared living expenses, even the purchase of a house or car, bank accounts, and/or insurance policies, you can find yourself open to all of the same kinds of claims that husbands make. Such claims are much less likely to stick outside of a marriage, but there is absolutely no guarantee that some judge somewhere won't find in favor of your live-in companion.

What can you do to protect yourself?

If you are contemplating marriage, by all means put in place a properly drawn pre-nuptial agreement that covers the kinds of concerns you'll have in your career and retirement. Even if you are already married without such a document, consult an attorney about drawing up a post-nuptial agreement for the same purpose.

The same holds true if you are simply living with someone: Consult your attorney and see what sort of document can be drafted to protect you from claims at a later time.

You should be aware of the latest statistics regarding separation and divorce. More than 60 percent of those married for the first time in the 1980s will divorce. The numbers are worse for second and third marriages. They are also somewhat worse if you lived with your husband prior to marrying him. In other words, the odds are against a tranquil, problem-free marital existence.

Most people would prefer not to deal with unpleasant subjects such as estate planning, drawing up a will, and getting a divorce, but this head-in-the-sand approach to things has a tendency to backfire. Those who recognize their own potential vulnerability and take legal steps to protect themselves always fare better.

Chapter 9

Retirement and Your Housing Needs

∾∾∾∾

Just How Safe Is This Annuity? Checking Your Policy

If you are concerned about your life insurance policy or annuity, here are some questions to ask: 1) Does your state have a guarantee fund? What is the limit? 2) What are the companies' ratings from A. M. Best, Moody's Investors Service and Standard and Poor's? Does your state insurance department have any information on the company?

—THE NEW YORK TIMES, DECEMBER 9, 1990

There are several types of real estate with which you are likely to become involved. The first is your home, your primary residence, which you will either rent or buy.

The second is a vacation home or summer home, which could become a retirement home.

The third is real estate for profit. You might invest in real estate purely to speculate or to house dependent children or parents or to house your own business.

YOUR HOME

Your home, or primary residence, carries a double investment on your part. First, there's the cost to you to rent or to buy, including down payment and monthly mortgage payments. Second, there is the emotional investment—the endless hours of arranging, decorating, gardening, generally providing comfort for you and your family. It is always difficult to look at the real estate, which also happens to be your home, as potentially your main financial investment and your main source of forced savings and your main source of income and borrowing power in an emergency and in retirement, but this is precisely what you need to do.

....

Using real estate as a retirement investment requires careful analysis.

....

Every generation has a different real-estate scenario. Our parents tended to buy cheap, stay put, and sell at the top of the market. When housing was plentiful and relatively inexpensive and there was a great deal of undeveloped land and desirable locations, it was moderately easy for a young person or young family to come up with the down payment for a modest dwelling. As the years went by, families tended to either stay where they were and improve the property or move possibly once to an upgraded house and then stay put. Basements became recreation rooms, garages became suites for aging parents, attics became dormitories for teenagers and college students.

With the advent of the baby boom and the enormous demand it generated for real estate, those who had bought in the 1930s and 1940s and even 1950s found they had an asset that had appreciated many times over. Mortgages were generally paid off rather than refinanced. The home equity loan was unknown. Middle-aged couples could plan for the time when they sold the family home, "made a fortune," and took the money for a comfortable retirement in Florida.

88

The generation now coming into middle age, though, is faced with an entirely different kind of situation. Those who bought homes near or at the top of the market in the late Seventies and Eighties, when the demand for housing seemed to know no end, may find themselves sitting with real estate that has been essentially flat in value for several years—or worse, has declined in value. Many people in the 1970s and 1980s bought and sold and moved frequently. They believed that real estate would simply keep going up and that they would keep trading up.

It is now the 1990s and the baby-bust generation, just behind the baby-boom generation, does not generate enough demand for real estate to maintain the inflated prices of the 1980s. In some regions of the country, real-estate values have dropped 25 percent and 30 percent in the last five years. Those who planned, like their parents, to retire on the pot of gold they would receive when they sold the family home may in fact be looking at an empty pot. And that's not the worst of it. There are many people who not only paid top dollar for their homes, but also took out a full mortgage *and* took advantage of home equity loans so that they were able to almost totally leverage their homes. Those in that group who then saw their properties begin to go flat and finally decline in value can find themselves today in a situation where the amount of the mortgage, combined with the home equity loan, greatly *exceeds* the current value of the house. Home equity loan payments, if not made, can lead to loss of that home. So not only do these people not have a major asset to cash in in middle age to fund their retirement, they often find themselves in a situation where as they enter their fifties and sixties, they have no assets and substantial debt. Foreclosures and personal bankruptcies among the middle class and upper middle class in this age group have grown all too common.

To backtrack a bit. While everyone wanted to get into

the real-estate market in the Sixties, Seventies, and Eighties, for the enormous growth it seemed to promise, in the Nineties, all of a sudden, renting has become a viable option. Because most urban and surrounding suburban areas are greatly overbuilt with cooperative and condominium buildings, landlords are offering extremely attractive deals, including up to 25 percent and 35 percent off published rents for desirable apartments and houses. In many cases, these landlords of both the apartments and the single-family houses are, in their current financial desperation, simply looking to cover their mortgage and utility costs.

While the wisdom of the Sixties, Seventies, and Eighties said that renting was throwing away money and that one should do whatever was necessary to raise a down payment in order to own real estate not just to live in but as one's major investment, those days are now definitely over.

THE SECOND HOME, THE SUMMER HOUSE, THE WEEKEND HOUSE, THE FUTURE RETIREMENT HOUSE

In the general affluence of the Seventies and Eighties, many people felt they could afford a seond home. Young people in their twenties and thirties bought vacation homes to share with their children on weekends and during vacations and the summer. People in their forties and fifties with no children or grown children sought a place that they could use in order to get away from job pressures or to "try out" for retirement; others were just looking for an investment. These are situations where owners used their houses only a couple of weeks a year (if that) and rented them out the rest of the time for income and the tax deductions.

Several changes in the tax law, however, have made this less attractive and harder to handle logistically.

Second homes can be wonderful getaways or trial tests for retirement communities or great places for your children to play, but the areas in which they are most frequently located are areas most vulnerable to economic slumps, particularly real-estate slumps.

Resorts, vacation areas, even previously heavily populated retirement havens are in fact optional in terms of second homes. When there is an economic downturn, second homes are hit first. The areas that are generally dependent on the people who occupy those homes part time are hit simultaneously. This has a cyclical effect, and it is not uncommon for values in resort and vacation areas to swing wildly with the economy.

Moreover, second homes, even in affluent times, have a nasty way of costing as much to carry as primary residences.

When economic times turn difficult and people begin to put these houses on the market en masse, the market becomes instantly glutted and depressed. All of the services in these communities that exist only to service this part-time population are hit as well. This further drives down real-estate values, since even the homes occupied by year-round residents become vulnerable then.

What does this all mean? Second homes should be bought with great caution and, if at all possible, when the market is down. Another option is to buy handyman specials, so that no matter what happens, you don't have a maximum investment in such a home.

....

Actually living in areas you are considering for retirement is important.

....

These second homes are, of course, also vulnerable to changes in your life. These could include your children going away to school, an aging parent moving in with you, a separation or divorce, or a disabling illness. Any of these factors can cause you to think twice about constantly transporting yourself to this second location, or even just going for the occasional weekend. In addition to the expense, there is the exhaustion that begins to set in with the long trips.

One also has to think about the fact that the very community that might have attracted you as a place for your children to spend vacations might for the very same reason be all wrong as a retirement location. Communities that are child-centered can rarely also be retirement- or senior-centered. Unfortunately, in our culture, teens and seniors are frequently intolerant of each other as well.

Perhaps the best solution for weekend or vacation housing is renting. Although there is always that sense that you are throwing away the money and that you are not building equity, that could all be a mirage anyway. Your equity in a vacation home is only as good as the economy.

Despite all of these warnings, it is good to actually live in areas you are considering for retirement someday. There is a time, probably sometime in your forties, when your orientation begins to shift. On the surface, it would appear to be a good idea to buy a second home, if you can afford it, in an area that looks especially appealing for retirement, with terrific facilities, wonderful weather, and other people your own age.

Again, I would caution to rent first in the area before buying. And it's a mistake to rent only for the summer. Many communities that are absolutely glorious in the summer are nearly unlivable in the winter. Consider taking a year-round lease in two or three communities in your late forties and early fifties to see how you like them during the various seasons.

The best reason to rent rather than buy, in my opinion,

is that our country's retired population is undergoing a shift out of "retirement areas" back to areas in or near their original primary residences. It might seem that retirement housing in Florida is a sure thing, absolutely immune to economic cycles, but it is not immune to psychological cycles within the older population.

As well as returning to original primary residences, many seniors are returning to the city, where they find a more idyllic setting than that offered by the vacation home. While most women, like men, seek to get away from the high expenses, hassles, and commutes that are a part of metropolitan living by leaving and heading for the hills, the beach, or the farm, there are those who do just the reverse. A woman in her early sixties, whom I'll call Susan, recently retired from her job as a hospital administrator in a small town in the Midwest. Susan had been planning for at least a decade to forget rest and relaxation and to seek out entertainment and intellectual stimulation in her retirement. With her good health, considerable savings, hospital pension, and Social Security, she made her move upon retirement to Houston. Susan made a considerable profit when selling her comfortable suburban home and she found that Houston had much to offer her in her retirement. First of all, she bought a small but centrally located condominium in a new apartment complex where a portion of the apartments were reserved for seniors. She set about joining several local museums, in each case taking a senior discount. She joined the local senior citizens' group and immediately took advantage of the substantial discounts offered seniors for the theater, the ballet, and the opera.

Although Susan had no particular need for medical or hospital services upon her arrival in Houston, she made herself known at a nearby major teaching hospital, where she did weekly volunteer work. Her next step was to become involved in a weekly reading group that met at the public library. And, as she had always been physically active, she enrolled at a local health club, again using her senior discount.

The move to Houston was perfect for her. She had long sought out what little cultural life there was available in her small town and had been craving deeper involvement. Her work with the hospital had given her a chance to travel to a number of major cities each year and she had been researching a retirement location for about ten years. She had notebooks on five cities in particular that interested her.

Susan's final decision in favor of Houston was in part because of the good weather, in part because of the availability of senior housing, and in part because of the excellent cultural amenities.

Budgeting carefully, always taking advantage of senior discounts, Susan has been able to live in fact for *less* than she did in her small town. Since senior transportation passes make it possible for her to get wherever she wants to go, really quite inexpensively, she no longer needs a car. And she does not miss having to heat her big old house.

THE ENTREPRENEUR'S REAL-ESTATE SOLUTION

The situation that I am about to describe would work for you as a young retired person, might work for one of your parents, and might work for one of your grown children who is still financially dependent.

If, rather than looking primarily for rest and relaxation and leisure in retirement housing, you are looking to make some money, you should explore the market in two-, three-, and four-family dwellings. Look in a clean, stable, safe, possibly ethnic area populated by a stable blue-collar population or a stable white-collar population of modest means. Find a reasonably priced dwelling. This kind of housing is plentiful on the outskirts of all major cities. Make the required down payment and take on a mortgage with the longest payout possible. Move into one of the units and rent the others.

You can establish this enterprise as a business where you pay yourself a salary and perhaps pay your spouse or companion a salary, too.

Before making any such move, though, have an engineer review the condition of the building and get the opinion of at least two real-estate experts, one banker, and one attorney on the viability of the neighborhood.

Further, it would be to your great advantage to buy a building that is already occupied with long-term happy tenants, where you simply continue their leases. Any empty building can be difficult to fill, plus there is probably some reason why it is empty to start with.

Such an arrangement can provide an invigorating atmosphere. Managing several units and handling the maintenance, upkeep, and finances can be a major activity and diversion for you and another.

If you fully analyze the economics of such a move in advance and are sure that the rents that you will take in will amply cover your mortgage, maintenance, utilities, taxes, and your own salary, this can be a very comfortable arrangement. If you have also bought into an area that is not over-built, and not in or headed toward a real-estate slump, you should be able to realize a profit on the building should you choose to sell it.

Another alternative is to take your earnings from the building and duplicate your effort with a second multifamily dwelling in the same neighborhood, which you could still easily monitor.

As I said earlier, this kind of arrangement can work for you, or you might wish to install a grown child or a parent in such an operation.

FLUCTUATING HOUSING NEEDS

Retired people are not a homogeneous group. They divide roughly into the early retirees, those in their fifties and early sixties; the middle retirees, those in their mid-sixties and seventies; and the elderly retirees, those starting at late seventies and early eighties.

....

Your changing needs in retirement include housing.

....

Young retirees more closely resemble people in their forties than people in their seventies. They tend to be active, involved, interested, easily bored. The stories are endless about people who couldn't wait to get on the golf course in Florida but after a year or two of it find their lives boring, empty, and disconnected and move back either into the communities where they always lived in their primary residence, or into communities near their children and grandchildren, or—increasingly—into communities where an employment opportunity presents itself.

Healthy retired people tend more often than not to seek some employment activity, either out of financial need, because their funds have run out quickly, or to enrich their lives. In many cases such employment is in an area they've always wanted to work in or worked in previously as a volunteer; sometimes it's in an area they know only through a hobby.

The main message in all of this is to be cautious, think

things through, and realize that if you retire in your fifties, you probably have three life cycles ahead of you, and your housing needs in any one of them could be quite different. The Maine woods that look appealing and full of adventure in your fifties might not look so perfect in your eighties. Keep your investments modest, well thought out. Don't put all your eggs in one basket.

No matter how good your financial planning, you have to keep in mind that our economy is no longer national but most certainly global. While there will be plenty of surprises, certain facts are inescapable. For one, the cost of energy is only going to go up. This means the cost of heating one's dwelling needs to be carefully studied. First of all, some dwellings are energy-efficient. This is a big plus. Homes in warm climates obviously use less heating fuel. On the other hand, homes in warm climates use more electricity to run air conditioners. As people grow older, they become more and more sensitive to shifts in heat and cold, and need to maintain a relatively stable temperature. This is going to be expensive one way or the other.

As people grow older, they also become increasingly dependent on the medical establishment—this is inescapable—and in more and more cases need to be near medical facilities not only for themselves, but also for their aging parents, who frequently move back in with them or become dependent on them. Retiring in an area where there are no available hospital beds and where there is a real strain on medical services would not be a good idea.

Make sure your real-estate moves enhance the general quality of your life and reduce rather than increase your anxiety level. Your aim is for an interesting, productive, joyous life.

At some point in your retirement or the retirement of your spouse or companion, you will reach the middle retirement age, a point where you desire some household assistance, which might mean housekeeping, cooking, help with dressing, help with errands and transportation. While there have always been nursing homes and "old age" homes for those who require medical assistance, either in minor matters or in major disabling matters, there is a new breed of housing that has been cropping up in the last ten years or so.

It is housing aimed at what I refer to as the middle-tier retirees—roughly, those between sixty-five and seventy-five. This is housing for people who are no longer employed or active in their own communities or households. It is housing that attempts to duplicate all of the comforts and privacy of home while at the same time opening up options that can be taken advantage of daily or occasionally. This housing tends to be near or associated with retirement areas and communities. It does not offer any medical assistance but may have an association with a nursing home or hospital, which is nearby. Three main types of operations are offered.

First, there are those that are strictly rental, pay as you go for as long as it's appropriate for you. These units tend to be aimed at the upper middle class. Individual apartments are offered with all of the amenities as well as certain conveniences aimed at people who have some difficulty getting around, perhaps because of arthritis or other ailments that tend to afflict people in this age group. Privacy is assured but company is also guaranteed, if sought, in the form of one or more communal meals a day. Appropriate recreational facilities are available. Housekeeping and personal maid services are generally available as well.

A second option is similar to standard condominiums, where you buy your unit and then pay for maintenance and the purchase, as needed, of any of the services offered by the organization.

A third option is more similar to a standard nursing home option in which you basically turn over your life savings and pay a flat down payment, and you are then guaranteed housing and care forever, first in this senior housing and later in a nursing home environment, if required. (Women in the third tier of retirement—roughly, ages seventy-five to ninety—will probably need at-home nursing services or a nursing home at some point.)

Another point that you must consider in your long-range real-estate planning is that because your life expectancy as a female is considerably higher than that of males, at some point in your life you will probably find yourself in a nearly all-female environment. Thus, in selecting retirement or senior housing for your later years, it would be a mistake to choose an establishment that offers services primarily for the husband, with services and activities for the wife being clearly secondary.

As you can see, the entire area of real estate in retirement is multifaceted, complex, and full of contradictions. Even if you get a fix, however, on the financial ramifications of all the possibilities, don't lose sight of the psychological factor. Human beings are social and need friends, companions, family, a support system. After careful consideration of the financial and business implications of all of your options, you may end up making your decision on the basis of companionship. There's nothing wrong with that. You should simply be informed when you make the decision.

I recall a situation I witnessed years ago that I thought was quite peculiar at the time, but now can appreciate. I worked with a man who was in his early sixties and nearing the company's mandatory retirement age of sixty-five. It turned out that he had been planning his retirement for ten years with seven other people—his wife and three other couples with whom they had played bridge for years. These four couples had been socially close for decades, taking vacations together, living in the same community. The man I knew, rather than waiting for exactly age sixty-five when he would have received the maximum pension benefits, opted to retire a couple of years early so that his retirement meshed with the others in his group. All eight of them did in fact move to a lovely community in South Carolina, which they had apparently visited during many vacations. Some of them had family nearby. It was in no way a retirement community, simply one that they found to be congenial to their main interests. The weather was pleasant, the housing was affordable, the community was historical, and there were important support services as well as cultural and medical facilities nearby. The well-laid plans of this retirement group paid off over the years in that they were able to meet their basic needs in early, middle, and late retirement within the structure of their group move.

Chapter 10

Retirement Planning and Insurance

~~~~

few subjects cause as much confusion, irritation, and frustration as that of insurance—finding it, buying it, maintaining it, qualifying for it, collecting on it.

The main purpose in your maintaining proper insurance is to help you spread the risk, cushion the blow, amortize the cost of difficulty and disaster. Proper insurance serves as a safety net.

If you are like most Americans, you may have too much life insurance and not enough, if any, disability, liability, property, and comprehensive health insurance.

Buying insurance is not something you should just "get out of the way." Maintaining proper insurance is a key category in your overall financial-planning strategy. Each type of insurance available serves a different purpose, and you must remember that your purposes will change dramatically during different phases of your life.

Your objective, in retirement, should be to have adequate coverage in all areas *and* to have it with strong and reputable insurance companies. The insurance industry is far flung and includes weak companies and strong companies. Before you make any purchases at all, you should discuss your insurance needs with your insurance broker, and possibly your attorney and accountant. The best way to find an insurance broker is through word of mouth. An insurance broker must be someone you trust, someone with experience, and someone who understands your real needs and desires and is eager to help you meet them. It also must be someone flexible, who's willing to update your insurance annually and to review it with you during any time of major change in your life.

··

Insurance can be one of the least-understood requirements in financial planning.

··

Once you have located an insurance broker, you need to give him or her a truthful and current picture of your financial and professional life, your responsibility for dependents, and your plan for your future. You don't want to be over-insured, buying more than you need, with overlapping benefits. On the other hand, you need to buy insurance with both your current and future needs in mind. For instance, it is obviously easier and cheaper to get life insurance and health insurance when you are young. You will probably find that some money spent then saves you money and difficulty at a later time.

GROUP OR INDIVIDUAL INSURANCE

Whenever possible, *always* participate in group insurance plans. If, at your corporation, union, or professional group, you are able to participate in health insurance, life insurance, or disability insurance plans, by all means do. First of all, the rates will almost certainly be lower than what you would pay as an individual. Second, the policy is apt to be better serviced, and you are apt to have fewer problems with claims if you are part of a large group policy, professionally monitored by both your employer and possibly an outside consultant. Importantly, if you joined these plans when you were relatively young, your inclusion may have been automatic or may have required a standard physical exam. All kinds of insurance are more difficult to get as you get older, and when you apply as an individual, the scrutiny is much greater and the motivation of the company to take you, much less. Finally, if you are fortunate enough to get it, you will, of course, pay more—possibly a great deal more—for your life insurance, disability insurance, and health insurance.

Not all insurance companies are equally strong. Some are currently on shaky ground because of poor management or poor investments. First of all, go to your local library and check out your insurance companies in *Best's Insurance Guide*. Only get involved with companies with the very highest ratings (if you have group policies, though, naturally you will have to stick with the choice of your employer or group).

When an insurance company is shaky, or under particularly great pressure to cut costs, one place they look first to make cuts is with individual policies. No matter what they charge for these, they are not as profitable to the insurance companies as group policies.

If you are currently employed and planning to leave the

company, by all means check into converting your group insurance to your own name. Perhaps this is already part of your earned retirement package, and your life insurance and health insurance coverage will continue either at your current coverage level or a reduced level. (It is unlikely that your disability insurance will continue.)

The COBRA law requires that employers who terminate employees make continued health insurance coverage available to them for up to eighteen months while they seek their own insurance.

In departing your company, the insurance issue can get murky if it's a choice between remaining with a weak or unreliable or unstable insurer who happens to carry the group insurance versus trying to take out an individual policy on your own with a stronger company. Seek the advice of a trusted insurance broker on this matter. You just can't forget that on your own you have very little leverage with these insurance companies, and you must rely on reputation, stability, reliability, and the *Best's* rating.

LIFE INSURANCE

There are dozens of variations on life insurance policies offered by perhaps hundreds of companies, but they fall primarily into a couple of categories. First of all there's term insurance. Term insurance pays a flat sum, on your death, to your estate or chosen beneficiary. Term insurance is renewable annually, and you can experience a rate increase at any renewal. You do not accumulate savings in a term policy, and you cannot borrow against it. It is, however, cheap. It is the least expensive form of insurance, and if your goal is simply to have a lump sum available at your death, this might be the best choice.

....

**It is important to seek the advice of an insurance broker
you trust and understand.**

....

Whole life insurance is another very popular kind of life insurance. Unlike term, which expires on a predetermined date, whole life is open-ended, and as long as the annual premiums are paid, it will remain in force. It does build savings, and you can borrow against it. Generally premiums do not increase.

Universal life is a variation on whole life, and an annual premium paid is essentially split between that amount needed to cover the cost of term-like insurance and the balance, which is invested on a tax-deferred basis and generally pays money market interest rates. The option exists with universal life to raise or lower premiums, which affects the savings portion of the policy. Variable life is yet another form of life insurance, similar to universal life, but riskier, and involves the actual policyholder handling the investment and savings portion of the funds.

Any group policy you have is almost certainly term insurance. Term insurance is easily understood and can be purchased by an individual with little or no outside help. Whole life, with its savings and investment element, and variable life policies are really primarily investment and savings instruments and should be considered as part of an overall savings and investment strategy and reviewed with a financial planner and/or accountant.

The consensus of consumer groups is that life insurance should pay a death benefit and that you should buy the cheapest insurance possible for that objective. These groups take the position that buying other forms of insurance may not be the best use of your money and they must be scrutinized and compared with other avenues available for savings and investing.

Whatever your decision, it can't be made without analyzing the impact of agents' and brokers' fees on various policies. Be sure to ask about this and get some sort of explanation in writing—one that you can understand!

How Much Life Insurance Do You Need?

The quick response to this, and the one probably given by the personnel director where you work, is an amount equal to one or two times your gross salary. Such a rule of thumb, while vaguely useful, is simply one guideline. The amount of life insurance you need is actually best calculated by assessing the total financial needs of your dependents, for as long as they will be dependent, less other funds available for their care. By way of example, if you have no adult dependents (spouse or aging parents) and only one child, age nineteen, a sophomore in college, you will most certainly want to have enough insurance to cover tuition and living expenses for the remaining three years of college for your child (technically, upon graduation your child should be self-supporting). If you have more than one child and they are much younger, and if you also have a partially dependent aging parent, you need to work out individual budgets for the care of each dependent. If, upon your death, in addition to life insurance, these dependents will have available to them the proceeds from a fully paid-for primary residence, possibly a secondary residence, a car, stocks, bonds, and annuities, then your life insurance may serve simply as a supplement to tide your dependents over for a year while the rest of your estate is dealt with.

If you have no dependents, there is some real question as to whether you need any life insurance at all and if any, possibly only enough for funeral and burial expenses.

Remember that you may have other types of insurance

that would come into play in the event of your death. You may have mortgage insurance, which will pay off the mortgage on your home. You may have insurance covering your investment portfolio. Don't double-insure. It's a waste of money.

Although, as you can see, calculating how much life insurance you need is a terribly complex task, if you are looking for an easy formula, in my opinion, you should carry an amount equal to three times your annual gross income. Three years' income should give the executors of your estate time to organize the affairs of your dependents in such a way as to maintain as well as possible the kind of lifestyle you provided to them through managing or selling assets and through investments.

How to Buy Life Insurance

If you do not have group coverage and wish to purchase your own insurance policy, you can buy either through an agent, who is the representative of an individual insurance company, or you can buy through a broker, who represents people who buy insurance. The agents, who are working for the insurance companies, work on a commission basis. They can be either exclusive agents, working for only one company, or non-exclusive, working for as many insurance companies as they choose.

Agents and brokers may or may not be certified. If they are, they generally have completed the required course by groups such as the Chartered Life Underwriters. You will need to check this on your own.

Every state has an insurance regulatory board which monitors the activities of all insurance companies based within that state. Any complaints you have regarding a particular insurer or agent or broker should be referred to your state agency. Some states, as you can imagine, do a better job than other states. If you are purchasing a lot of insurance, it might be wise to check into the protection available to you as a resident of your state.

One thing you will surely find when shopping for insurance is that different companies charge different rates for seemingly identical policies. They are free to do so. While they all use actuarially generated information to set rates, this is only part of the process. Each company has its own financial objective and may in fact want to expand one particular kind of business and cut back on another, and the company's rate structure will reflect this. Tedious as it is, you should absolutely comparison-shop when buying any kind of insurance.

Note: Even if you are not currently employed, you need life insurance if you have dependents. You may have a spouse who is working, but in the event of your death, your spouse and dependents would have to cover the costs of your services as a homemaker, mother, and caregiver for dependent parents. That cost is extremely high.

Life Insurance as a Gift

If you are certain that you have an adequate amount of life insurance to cover the financial needs of your dependents (generally in conjunction with disposition of your other assets), you may wish to increase your life insurance amount anyway as a "gift" to your beneficiary upon your death. You certainly can do this. However, this might not be the best way to leave such an asset. You are now talking about investing in life insurance for a future return on your money. This is investing. This requires an investment adviser. I would not rely on an insurance agent to make this decision for you. This really falls into the area of estate planning, and estate planning is one facet of financial planning that is best done with financial advisers such as a lawyer, an accountant, a portfolio manager, or a banker.

HEALTH INSURANCE

If you are employed full time by a corporation, you almost certainly have group health insurance. A generation ago, your company may have paid the entire cost for this insurance and you may have been lulled into thinking that your group insurer simply paid your health-care bills. Perhaps your employer asked for no contribution from you, the coverage was wide, and claims were paid quickly and efficiently.

....

Our fluctuating economy makes individual health-care planning a necessity.

....

The situation in health care is greatly changed. First of all, approximately 35 million Americans have no health insurance at all. Almost all others, whether part of a group plan or self-insured, are encountering difficulties. The cost of health care and consequently the cost of health insurance has skyrocketed in the last decade. The combination of an aging population, new and expensive advanced medical techniques, and the AIDS epidemic has rendered the cost of health insurance coverage out of reach for many. Corporations, which have long offered comprehensive health insurance to their employees, have been systematically reducing that overall coverage, while increasing the amount of deductibles and the contribution required by employees for the coverage. In addition, physical examinations are becoming more comprehensive. For those seeking insurance on their own, the cost is truly outrageous and the number of companies willing to write individual policies is diminishing.

Since Americans have always considered health insurance as something of a birthright, these changes over the last decade have aroused enormous consumer rage. There is a great deal of pressure on Congress to pass some kind of national health insurance coverage program, similar to that available in almost all other industrialized countries. Even if a universal, comprehensive program for all Americans is not made available shortly, there are sure to be some inroads made. Already, "pared back" policies are cropping up that offer only minimal coverage, but at much lower rates, to individuals and small businesses in particular. Moreover, corporations have begun to invest in "wellness" programs that offer substantial incentives to employees to stop smoking, start exercising, control their weight, and eliminate the use of dependency-related substances.

As you plan your retirement, arranging for adequate health insurance coverage should be a top priority. In fact, you should make no move on the employment, real-estate, or recreational fronts until you have adequate insurance of all types.

In health insurance, you have a number of options. If you are employed, you should carefully examine your policy to see if you need supplemental coverage in order to meet your needs for the next several decades. If you do, make an application for such a policy immmediately through your trusted broker or agent. Of course, if you are in good health and fitness, you will have an easier time getting this coverage. If you find the cost of personal individual health insurance too prohibitive, you should look into health maintenance organizations and variations on them, including PPOs (preferred provider organizations). These alternative forms of insurance tend to stress prevention. I happen to think this is all well and good and, for most people, will probably lead to fewer medical expenses and fewer medical needs. HMOs, for a reasonable annual fee, do of course require that you use their doctors and facilities, including laboratories. If you find this acceptable, this kind of coverage should make sense for you. HMOs sometimes are criticized for not pursuing all tests available for a particular complaint and not permitting long enough hospital time, although these complaints tend to refer to individual operations. The preferred provider organizations permit you, for somewhat higher fees, to combine their doctors and facilities with your doctors and facilities. Since good health is such an over-whelming concern in your retirement, do not make this decision quickly. Investigate all options available to you, their cost to you, and the coverage they provide for your needs now as well as those needs you anticipate having in the future. Again, as with life insurers, you need to carefully research the stability and reputation of any health insurers you're seriously considering.

Health insurance offers so many options that you need to carefully calculate the tradeoffs involved in deductibles and fees allowable for procedures, prescriptions, lab tests, hospital stays, and doctors' exams.

Perhaps you are now fifty or sixty and feel that this is not a terrible worry since Medicare kicks in for you at age sixty-five, when you start collecting Social Security benefits. That is giving you a false sense of security. Medicare does not cover everything. You would do well to go to your local Social Security office and pick up a copy of their brochure titled simply "Medicare." In fifteen pages, this brochure de-scribes in great detail exactly what is and what is not avail-able through Medicare.

The important thing to remember is that health insur-ance is your own personal responsibility. When selecting a new health insurer or supplementing coverage you already have, you must keep in mind your own current health, the health history of your family, and the availability of doctors and medical facilities in your area.

If you have had one family physician for your entire adult life and have depended on his or her advice on all matters related to your health, by all means discuss this matter of insurance with your physician as well.

Medicaid

Medicaid is a form of health insurance available to those participating in public-assistance programs. It is extremely difficult to meet the qualifications for this program. You should not make it part of your planning. Hopefully you'll never need it.

Cost of Health Insurance

In the maze known as health care, you need to be particularly diligent about checking these items:

1. Annual cost to you.

2. Provisions regarding cost increases or cancellation.

3. Portion of expense covered or maximum allowable for services, lab tests, doctors' fees, hospital stays.

4. Is psychiatric care covered at all, and if so, under what restrictions?

5. Are substance-abuse-related medical costs covered, and with what restrictions?

6. Are there maximum amounts available for particular diseases? Or perhaps maximum amounts per year for these diseases?

7. Will your coverage continue after age sixty-five?

8. When will you receive your benefits payment and how will payment be made and to whom?

9. Is there any dental coverage at all, and with what restrictions?

10. Is home health care and nursing care covered?

11. Should you consider MEDIGAP insurance to supplement your medicare insurance?

If you make a comprehensive list of the costs of all of the health insurance coverage you would like and then calculate the total cost, chances are it will not be affordable. Whether you are planning to convert your insurance where you work or to seek an individual private health insurance plan, you will have to pick and choose and make some compromises regarding your coverage. The first area open to your scrutiny is that of deductibles. You may think that you want little or no deductible, but the cost of a low deductible might be beyond your reach. Remember, health insurance is really not there to pay all of your medical bills, it is there to spare you the unbearable price of unexpected and enormous medical costs. Let's say your income is $50,000 to $75,000 a year. You really could afford a deductible of even $1,000. There is a big difference between insurance with a $200 deductible and insurance with a $1,000 deductible. If you view your medical insurance as emergency insurance, you can get your premiums way down.

If you've made a list of the comprehensive services you want covered and you've included both dental and psychiatric, you may have in fact doubled your annual premium. First of all, dental needs rarely present a life-threatening emergency, and you may simply have to plan to cover your own dental expenses on an as-needed basis, with concentration on your part on preventative measures.

The areas of psychiatric coverage and coverage for disability caused by substance abuse are very tricky. Insurance companies take a very hard look and disallow many expenses in these areas even when you may feel the coverage should pay for everything. In the psychiatric area, for instance, expenses run the gamut from private, hourly-fee-based services of licensed psychiatrists all the way down to group therapy sessions by psychologists. Be absolutely certain what the policy you have in mind will cover, and be sure you want to pay the extra premium for this coverage.

PROPERTY INSURANCE

You have spent your working life paying for and accumulating personal possessions. These possessions include your primary residence, any secondary residence, your automobile, perhaps a boat, furniture, clothing, silver, china, fine art, furs, jewelry, collectibles, and so on.

When you consider that it could take you another entire working lifetime to accumulate these possessions again, you can see the absolute wisdom in having adequate property insurance. First of all, you want to insure your home. If you own it, you want to insure the actual structure as well as the possessions inside it. Both should be insured at replacement value. Insuring it for its value at the time of purchase is inadequate if the scenario you most wish to avoid is serious property loss in a situation where your insurance only covers your original cost, less depreciation. Although the premiums are higher, it is well worth it to insure the structure of your home and everything in it for replacement value. I strongly recommend replacement-value insurance for *all* of your possessions. With fine-arts coverage and other special coverage, such as for jewelry, silver, and furs, you will find that you need supplementary insurance to your basic homeowner's insurance.

If you rent, insurance is just as important, except you do not need to insure the value of your rented house or apartment since you don't own it. But you do need to insure, at replacement value, everything in it.

Good record keeping will pay off later, whether you file a small claim, perhaps for water damage, or an enormous claim, perhaps for the loss of your entire home and its possessions in a fire.

An excellent way to keep track of what you own is to do a videotaped inventory of your home. Do every room, and, with the camera running, go in closets and in drawers. As you mention each item, give its approximate value if possible, and if a serial number is visible, read it during your videotaping. If you photograph your valuables, there are special albums for storing the pictures. Do not keep these in your home, however, unless you have a safe or a fireproof box.

Keep a complete record of the sales receipts, canceled checks, and credit-card monthly billing statements listing all significant purchases. This is best kept in your safe-deposit box. I recommend that twice a year you do a video supplement where you again go room to room but this time only picking up recent purchases.

In the case of works of art, be certain to individually tape each. When you do your jewelry, take it out of the jewelry box and lay it on a table so that each piece can be seen. When you do your clothing closet, pull major items such as furs out and videotape separately.

When you do your first videotape record for insurance purposes, do your own rough estimate of the replacement cost of everything in your home. This would provide at least a guideline, in conjunction with sales receipts and the video, for the insurance company in the event of a claim.

Remember that you may have important possessions outside of your home as well. If you own your primary residence but rent a secondary residence, carry full insurance on the possessions in the secondary rental. Also, if you are accustomed to keeping your own furniture, artwork, or equipment at your office, follow exactly the same procedure there.

Once you've completed your record, review it with your insurance broker and seek his or her opinion on whether you need to supplement it in any way with additional records.

AUTOMOBILE INSURANCE

It would be best to seek your insurance broker's recommendation regarding the proper amount of automobile insurance for you. The amount depends on the age and condition of your automobile, its make, your location (major cities are especially expensive), whether it is personally or professionally garaged, whether it is leased or owned, whether you have had automobile insurance claims in the past, the state in which you reside, your age, your driving record, and the use to which you intend to put your vehicle, whether it is business, pleasure, or a combination of both.

Your state law dictates certain insurance coverage that you must have; other coverage will be at your discretion. Automobile insurance is extremely expensive, so analyze the situation carefully and buy only what you need.

LIABILITY INSURANCE

The purchase of personal liability insurance will allow you to sleep easier. This insurance covers you in the event of a claim against you by someone who holds you responsible for injury to them. Since most such occasions are totally unexpected and can lead to vast expense in terms of legal fees and damages paid, it is wise to carry a sizable amount of personal liability insurance. This insurance is not expensive and simply provides a safety net for you. Talk with your insurance broker regarding your specific needs, especially related to your residence, place of business, and professional risk.

Umbrella liability insurance policies provide you with coverage beyond that which your own medical and homeowner policies cover. For a relatively low fee, you can get as much as a million dollars' or more excess coverage.

when they can no longer do it for a salary, they do it as a volunteer. And there are others who have lived one kind of life, never happily, and have been patiently waiting for the opportunity to switch gears entirely. I have a female friend who feels that she has fulfilled her obligations to her now-grown children, as well as her near-retirement husband, and she has just enrolled in divinity school.

My own mother appears to be in at least the third cycle of her adult life. She had a traditional marriage, raised three children, and then decided to continue her education; afterward, she took an entry-level position in a corporation and rose by age sixty-five to assistant treasurer of the corporation. After about ten days of "retirement," she launched herself into local politics; she also teaches an aerobics course at her local health club and has started a part-time sales career in publishing as well. And I notice that she plays more golf and goes dancing more often than she did in her forties!

HEALTH AND FITNESS

It may be that at one time retired women did spend a lot of time in rocking chairs knitting by the fire. Then again, that may never have been the case, but the image certainly sticks in our minds. Such a sedentary existence would certainly have shortened those women's lives.

The evidence is overwhelming that moderate exercise and careful diet keep women vigorous into their eighties and nineties. In selecting a location for your retirement, you must factor in availability of fitness facilities or a congenial atmosphere in which you can at least walk, possibly bicycle, swim—whatever your preference.

At some point, it will also become important to you that the older people with whom you are surrounded share your outlook on retirement. If it is your hope to be physically active and vigorous and involved, you need to assess if that is the general lifestyle of the retired and older people in the area of your choice.

Exercising the mind will be equally important. Easy access to cultural and entertainment and even advanced educational facilities will make a difference. This poses one of the quandaries of selecting a retirement site. A major city may offer opera, ballet, the symphony, and museums, but virtually no suitable transportation or housing, and the medical facilities could be crowded or, in fact, overwhelmed.

An interesting alternative is a university community or a community near a university. The physical surroundings can be quite congenial, comfortable, and affordable, while at the same time the university will probably be the site of a variety of cultural, entertainment, and intellectual activities.

As the importance of age decreases and the importance of mental and physical vitality increases, you need to think carefully about whether you wish to spend your retirement decades in an environment filled mostly with people your age or in a more diverse spread. This is a complex question. Older people are always happy to be rid of teenage noise and the potential of vandalism, not to mention the chaos often present with small children, but in many cases they later regret having traded protection from those elements for a sterile environment. There is mounting evidence that retired people enjoy interaction with all age groups. It's fair to say that retired people would like to have a social and political impact on their environment, and even dominate it, but not at the expense of withdrawal from the larger community.

As the baby-boom generation, a huge population bubble, passes into middle age, they are apt to set a new tone for retirement, the way they have for so many other things because of their large numbers. First of all, they most likely will define middle age as starting at sixty rather than forty— and old age as eighty-five rather than sixty-five. They will influence everything, including advertising and television images that define who we are and what we are supposed to be like and look like. There will be far more programs with stars like Angela Lansbury than those with twenty-year-old models. Communities will be under pressure to give equal weight to the needs of those over fifty as those under eighteen. Community and state budgets, which traditionally give priority to the education of the young, will be forced to share the funds available with the over-fifty population, whose needs will most certainly include housing, transportation, and the availability of leisure and educational facilities.

With all of these considerations, how can one possibly decide on the best possible area for retirement? The trick is to decide, first of all, whether you intend to retire at all voluntarily and, second, whether you want to escape your current location or would prefer to find a way to stay there forever. Do you draw pleasure and companionship and support from family, neighbors, and fellow employees, or is that not an issue with you? It could be that your children live three thousand miles away, or you have no children and you have only lived where you live in order to be near your employment, which you are looking forward to terminating.

A retirement location is an entirely personal decision. What works for one person can be a total disaster for another.

Furthermore, don't think of yourself as a retired person at fifty or sixty. Think of that as sort of a preretirement time, or modified retirement time, and view the needs you have then separately from those you are likely to have in your seventies, eighties, and nineties. Lay a plan, explore all of your options, but don't close the door on returning to your current residence location if an experiment in another area does not work out.

RETIRING TO A FOREIGN COUNTRY

You may have vacationed in Mexico (or Greece or London) and loved it so much that you've decided your goal is to live there when you retire. This is a decision that has serious ramifications. First of all, on the positive side, it might be that you have found a location where you can maintain the lifestyle to which you are accustomed, on a much lower income. It may be appealing to find a wonderful house, a stimulating culture, and day-to-day living expenses that are half what you have now.

These are some questions that you need to think about, however.

1. Do you speak the language?

2. Do you have a guaranteed income? (The likelihood of finding employment in a foreign country at retirement age is slim.)

3. Is this country politically stable, or on the verge of revolution or other social/political upheaval?

4. Is this country in a deep economic slump, and is that the reason things are cheaper? Would a change in the political climate greatly increase your expenses?

5. What is the cultural attitude toward women, especially women living alone?

If you have simply vacationed in a country, you may not have a real fix on what living there would be like. In many foreign countries, the political and religious attitudes toward women would make your existence there on a full-time basis unpleasant. While you may be welcome everywhere in this fine country in the presence of your husband, what will happen if you are there alone?

If you are close to family and friends, seeing them could be a problem, as travel to a foreign country might be either too time-consuming or too expensive for them. Furthermore, they might not find the new culture to be as appealing as you do. Have you checked out the regulations concerning taxation—national, local, real estate, school? Are foreigners allowed to buy residential property? Are foreigners allowed to establish businesses? What will the status of your health coverage, insurance coverage, pension payments, and annuity payments be?

If you have carefully weighed all of these questions and are still seriously considering moving to another country, exercise great caution. Rent a house in the country, in the specific area in which you would be likely to live. Occupy it for an entire year so that you can see seasonal changes. Do not sell your primary residence in the United States. Make some other arrangement, such as renting it furnished for a year so that if after that year you've changed your mind, you will not have closed out your other main housing option. You should have no trouble finding a tenant for your primary residence in the United States. You might not make money on the deal, but you also shouldn't lose any.

Living abroad for a year could be a wonderful adventure, even if you do make the decision not to retire there permanently. This could be a very appealing course of action. In fact, it could be so appealing that you might try it several times in different countries, not so much to set up permanent retirement residency as to experience each new culture year-round. This is a much more relaxed and natural way to visit another country anyway, rather than taking a one- or two-week vacation at a hotel occupied primarily by tourists.

If you and your husband, or you and a companion of

your choice, are making this move together, it is possible—perhaps even likely—that only one of you will like the change. Your ultimate decision not to move abroad might be based on the fact that the relationship is more important than an overseas move, and you may look to some sort of residential compromise to preserve the relationship.

··

Be flexible in your plans, but keep your retirement goals clear and focused.

··

When I first moved to New York City, I worked with a woman who was planning to take early retirement at about age fifty. She had lived in New York all of her life and was planning a big change. Unlike most women planning retirement, however, she was not looking for perfect weather, new job opportunities, senior housing, or convenient health-care facilities. She was unabashedly looking for men! I worked in an office near hers for about two years and she frequently gave me an update on her plans. She said New York was terrific in lots of ways, but in her opinion the men were a disaster. First of all, there weren't enough of them, and second of all (again, in her opinion), those who were there had delusions regarding their own worth because of supply and demand. At any rate, her research showed that there were in fact a number of cities in the United States where the male/female ratio was either one to one, or two to one, or even three to one. Most of those places tended to be in Wyoming and Montana, but she personally had settled on Anchorage, Alaska. She informed me that in Anchorage there was the highest number of males per female of any city in the United States at that time. I could think of few places worse to retire to than Anchorage with its subzero temperatures most of the year, but weather was not a factor for her. She was planning to marry. She had never been married and it was her goal to marry by age fifty-two.

She had no trouble finding a job in Anchorage. She visited several times prior to her retirement move. New York–trained administrative assistants, such as herself, were in short supply there, and her college education and sophisticated style were rarely matched.

All of us were absolutely stunned when she actually went through with her plans. She sent us monthly letters at the office and there was no question that she was having a dazzling social life, almost immediately upon arrival. And she met her objective. She married, not two years later, but less than one year later. This was all quite some time ago, and she is still there, still married to the same man, and having a very satisfying life.

Part Three

OBSTACLES IN RETIREMENT AND HOW TO PREPARE FOR THEM

□ Chapter 12 □

Your Changing Expenses

~~~~~~~

Going Beyond Social Security

Social Security typically replaces only about 30 percent of preretirement income.

—THE NEW YORK TIMES, MARCH 9, 1991

It is a widely held belief that your living expenses in retirement will be equal to about two-thirds your living expenses before retirement. While that is a useful rule of thumb, it masks the important point that the *way* in which you spend your money in retirement is apt to be dramatically different from the way you spent it prior to retirement.

....

In retirement, income doesn't need to be an elusive commodity.

....

You will continue to have short-term and long-term goals. In your younger years, your long-term major goals may have been buying a home, financing the college education of your children, and starting your own business. At retirement, you may already have your house paid for. Your children are educated. You may not have gotten around to starting your own business but might wish to now.

The large portion of your income that used to go for

your mortgage, home furnishings, and automobiles might be largely eliminated. You own your home, it is completely furnished, you have all the china, silver, and crystal you'll ever need, and you own two cars, which get very little use now that you don't have to drive thirty miles to and from work every day. While it's true that things do wear out and you may have an ongoing desire for high-tech electronic equipment, or you may like to totally redecorate every three years or so, this is a matter of personal preference rather than need. This category, which probably represented a very large chunk of your budget in your twenties, thirties, and forties, can be cut back to the bare essentials in later years.

Businesswomen, like businessmen, are expected to be dressed appropriately for their business day. Some businesswomen even spend several hundred dollars per outfit for office attire. Very few businesses provide any kind of wardrobe allowance, although there are exceptions for women who are expected to speak publicly and make TV or press appearances. This is probably a major expense for businesswomen prior to retirement.

In retirement, however, this is unquestionably an expense that can be reduced rather drastically. Even if one is still working part time, or starting one's own business, the necessity to be dressed exquisitely and expensively every day, year round, will be reduced.

Also, there is the factor of time. Businesswomen, again like businessmen, claim that they spend as much as they do on clothes because they have no time to shop for bargains, or even options. Businesswomen and businessmen frequently buy the same outfit in a couple of different colors or fabrics because it looks good and requires no further time or thought.

While I think it is sheer nonsense that women like to shop more than men, in retirement both have more time to review clothing options and to buy off-season. Leisure clothing is, of course, frequently less expensive than office attire at any time of the year.

And yet despite all of this, there are new expenses for retirees. If you have spent your career in a corporation and risen to a reasonably high level, you may very well have been one of those people who "live on their expense account." Think about this.

Are you or are you accustomed to:

- Eating out only if it is a business expense?

- Attending social and sporting events only if you take a client?

- Vacationing only as part of a business-related trip?

- Using only the car provided by the company?

- Making full use of the mailroom, copy machine, and office support staff provided by the company?

- Periodically having a clothing and grooming (hair and makeup) allowance because of radio/TV/public appearances for your job?

With these considerations in mind, your expenses in retirement must be viewed in two ways: first, those that will continue exactly the same as prior to your retirement, and those that will be either added or eliminated (it's the added expenses that are the hidden problem). Basically, your expenses will break down into the following:

HOUSING

You have a number of alternatives as far as housing goes. One, you can stay exactly where you are and continue to pay whatever you are paying (although it may be that as you approach retirement you have neared the point where you will have paid off your mortgage—though maybe not, since this is the case far less frequently now than it was a generation ago). The second alternative is to sell your current primary residence and move into your weekend or vacation home. A third alternative is to sell your primary and, where appropriate, secondary residences and move to an entirely new location, perhaps into a condominium rather than a house. Also at issue is whether you buy or rent.

As we discussed elsewhere in the book, an ever-increasing segment of the retired population has found that distant moves frequently do not work out. Retired people miss their peer group, colleagues, friends, and family. Retired people also frequently find that the very thing they sought—a homogeneous group of people approximately their own age—is not satisfactory. The sounds of children and even teenagers (a group they originally hoped to eliminate from their surroundings) can be missed.

Areas that are terrific on weekends or even summer vacations may seem grim and deserted year round. These vacation areas usually have economies that are seasonal, and if it is your intention to work part time, sufficient opportunities may not be available.

Your home may seem too large once your family has grown or moved. Beware! Before you go selling your large house and moving into a one- or two-bedroom residence, remember that retired, middle-aged people are increasingly being asked to take in *their* retired, aging parents. In addition to that trend, recent and not so recent college graduates tend to return home when the economy is down and they are unable either to find a job or to find one that covers the cost of independent housing. And, with the divorce rate hovering at 50 percent, recently divorced children and dependent grandchildren have been known to move in for a while as well.

Combine this with the surge in the number of women

starting their own small businesses in retirement, and you see that you may have many uses for the extra rooms. Many small businesses can be successfully launched and run even long term out of a garage, a family room, or an extra bedroom or two.

Since all of these possibilities could occur in one's retirement, perhaps the more prudent course of action is to simply close off the extra rooms or area of the house. Often it is the cost of heating or air conditioning those areas that is the real expense. If heat, electricity, and water are cut off when you close off an area, you will find your overall expenses significantly reduced.

As an alternative, and while you are deciding what to do next, you might consider contacting your local college or university. They are often looking for student housing and you could try, at least for a semester, renting part of your house to a student. This will bring in a little money, will probably cover your heating, cooling, and water expenses, and will buy you another nine months' time to think.

Another possibility, particularly if you live in a metropolitan area, or in an area where several large conglomerates have national headquarters, is to inquire about "corporate renting," whereby you would make available to the corporation a room, with use of the bathroom. In most cases, cooking facilities aren't required, as the room is usually for an executive who has to be at the headquarters only one or two days a month; still, the company feels a full-scale rental or hotel bill would be too much. You usually have the same person staying there, rather than different ones, and at most they will ask to leave a few changes of clothes in a drawer or closet. You might even inquire at your own corporation, particularly if your departure is the result of downsizing, whether this is something they'd be interested in; they might be only too pleased to cut out the company apartment or large hotel bills.

If you have retired very recently, the best course of action regarding housing may be no action at all. This is the sort of advice frequently given to women who panic financially as well as emotionally at the death of a spouse. Attorneys, bankers, and accountants all advise newly widowed women to "wait and see." Such advice seems to me to be applicable for retirees as well.

....

Using real estate creatively can produce unexpected benefits.

....

You have to remember that retirement has different stages: early retirement, when your needs are most likely aligned with non-retirees; middle retirement, when you most probably will have eliminated or seriously cut back any kind of employment; and late retirement, when your needs could be dramatically different from what they were in the first two stages, in that you may require special help (most commonly, household or medical assistance).

If you have an overwhelming desire to travel or make some big change in your life immediately upon retirement, consider renting your primary residence to others for a year or so while you explore your options.

TRANSPORTATION

If you currently have a company car, you have to expect to add on to your post-retirement expense list the cost of your own car—payments for car purchase or lease, gas, maintenance, and insurance.

If you have spent many years commuting to work, you have probably had the cost of an automobile, gas, insurance, parking, and possibly fares for public transportation such as trains and taxis as well. You may have had these expenses five days a week. If you are married, your spouse may have had identical expenses, and you may have required two cars as well.

In retirement, your transportation needs could change dramatically. If you are simply cutting back on your employment—going to the office perhaps two days a week and working one day at home—you can assume that your overall costs will drop by about one-third. You won't have the parking, and the train and taxis, but you will still have to make your car payments and insurance payments. You may find, however, that your family requires only one car rather than two.

At the same time that you have this kind of saving, you may have an enormous increase in the cost of airline tickets. Perhaps you were one of those people who only took vacations at the tail end of business trips, when your company was picking up the cost of the flight. You may have gone, for instance, to California or London or Paris several times a year and never really thought about the cost. Flying on your own money is expensive, though the cost can be reduced, of course, by taking advantage of special rates for seniors, where available, and buying tickets in advance.

VACATIONS

Again, if you were accustomed to taking vacations at the tail end of business trips, your cost of lodging might have been minimal—perhaps a few extra days at your own expense in a hotel where you were already booked at a corporate rate. This will of course change. You will be paying the full price (except where special senior discounts are available).

The best way to counter this increased cost is to take

your vacations off-season. Preretirement, you may have had to schedule vacations to coordinate with business trips or during the season when your company felt they could do without you (the summer), and that might have been the time when rates were highest. Off-season travel has many, many advantages, only one of which is the reduced cost. Another major plus is that, naturally, there are fewer people traveling off-season, and virtually no families with children (who are tied to school vacation schedules).

....

Consider preretirement benefits carefully and determine how to replace them with a limited or fixed income.

....

Another interesting option open to you in retirement is trading homes with another retired person or couple, either in another part of the country or abroad. The whole business of trading homes for a vacation is appealing to many who in the end decide against it because of the prospect of someone else's children in their home. When it is one retired couple switching with another retired couple, that particular difficulty is eliminated.

FOOD

Many working women, especially those who travel a great deal for their businesses, rarely, if ever, eat out on their own money. In the current business environment, it is easy to fall into a pattern of business breakfasts, business lunches, business cocktails, and business dinners. While this used to be a five-day-a-week phenomenon, it is frequently seven days a week now.

Women accustomed to a travel and entertainment budget of $5,000, $10,000, even $20,000 or $30,000 a year, quickly forget what it would be like to have to pay to dine in exquisite restaurants on their own money.

Many businesswomen haven't seen the inside of a supermarket in years. The fact that it now can cost several hundred dollars to fill up a shopping cart with bare necessities can come as a shock to someone who has never budgeted any significant amount of money for personal food consumption.

In many businesses, corporations also cover the complete cost of entertaining at home. Businesswomen who have one or two dinner parties and perhaps two major cocktail parties at home a month could easily be spending another several thousand dollars with caterers. To duplicate that on one's own can take a sizable chunk out of a retirement budget.

In addition, until recently, when the economy turned down, expense accounts were in many cases not very closely scrutinized. No one really questioned whether you needed to spend a hundred dollars or more for two people for lunch when the same business probably could have been transacted for half of that or maybe even less.

Executive women are not accustomed to scouting out inexpensive restaurants, and this can be a whole new adventure in retirement. It is hard to give up the habit of eating out a lot. Retired businesswomen may also have amnesia as far as cooking skills.

This whole area deserves careful consideration because the amount of money at stake is more than it appears.

ENTERTAINMENT

When was the last time you actually thought about the cost of two theater tickets, orchestra seats, or four ballet tickets, or a box at the opera? If these experiences have been a regular part of your life, chances are you wrote it off on your expense account.

Women in corporate life, or on Wall Street, or in politics are expected to entertain clients in exactly the same way men have always done. This can be one of the more pleasurable aspects of corporate life, although too much of it can become monotonous. Nevertheless, it is an expensive aspect. Perhaps a thousand dollars a year at the opera, another thousand at the ballet, and maybe even more than that at the theater, on top of restaurant expenses and car services, can add up to a very significant amount of money. Most women in retirement will not be willing to spend their own money to keep up this aspect of their lives. Of course, the responsibility to entertain clients might be gone, but the desire to stay culturally on top of things won't. Opera, theater, ballet, major sports events all have to be carefully budgeted. In a tight retirement budget, you have to remember that these items are, in fact, optional. And of course there are seats other than those in the orchestra.

In addition, you may have enjoyed a country club membership for many years, courtesy of your employer. When you joined the club, perhaps the annual dues were two thousand dollars and you really haven't paid much attention to it since. This is an expense you will now have to assume yourself if you wish to continue your membership, and the dues could be five or ten times what they were when you joined.

INSURANCE

In your business life, you may have had corporate life insurance, corporate health insurance, and corporate disability insurance, though in recent years there has been a move away from covering all or most of an employee's insurance expenses. You may have experienced in your own company a situation where you were asked to begin to pay part of your health insurance expense, for instance. Your company may have changed its policy on life insurance, and instead of insuring you at twice your salary, it may have been cut to the amount of your salary. And chances are, if you ever had disability insurance at all, it has been eliminated altogether.

In retirement, you could find your insurance needs dramatically changed. First of all, if your company has been acquired, has downsized, or has gone into bankruptcy, you may have trouble continuing any insurance coverage.

If you are one of the fortunate ones, though, and your corporation continues to maintain some health and life insurance for you during your retirement, you should review it carefully anyway. Chances are that what seemed like quite enough at age thirty or forty could be not at all adequate at fifty, sixty, seventy, or beyond. Most probably, you will have to supplement your insurance coverage, at a fairly stiff price to you.

If you find yourself uninsured, you, like close to 30 percent of all Americans, may be unable to get any kind of insurance at all. The United States is one of the few industrialized nations in the world that does not offer universal government-sponsored health insurance, though pressure is currently on Congress to provide something, and that may be available in the not too distant future.

Medicare and Medicaid are of course available under certain circumstances, and are discussed elsewhere in this book in more detail.

OUTSTANDING DEBT

You probably have some personal bank debt as well as credit-card debt, even if your mortgage is paid off. It would be wise to maintain current payments on this debt and attempt to gradually reduce it to zero. Buying on credit cards is really a convenience, and a very expensive one. Interest on these credit-card payments, which was once tax deductible, is no longer. The same is true of personal bank debt. Borrowing at the bank to go on vacation, or to cover the cost of Christmas presents, should become a thing of the past.

Chapter 13

Funding for Retirement

꩜꩜꩜

U.S. Lists Top Pension Plans at Risk
Weak companies may not be able to meet obliga-
tions to some plans.

The nation's fifty largest under-financed pension plans
have a potential combined shortfall of more than $14 bil-
lion, the Pension Benefit Guarantee Corporation said to-
day. Over 50 percent of the under-financing on this list
are either probable or possible losses.

—THE NEW YORK TIMES, FEBRUARY 26, 1991

One of the most difficult obstacles in retirement is ac-
quiring and maintaining the funds you will need to have the
lifestyle you desire. The following are some of the sources of
income from which you will most likely draw for your expenses, as well as detailed explanations of what these
sources can and cannot do for you.

PENSION PLANS

Twenty-three percent of women who work outside of the
home now receive some type of pension, while twice as
many men receive pensions. The main reason for the dispar-
ity is the multiplicity of roles that women carry. Most wom-
en, even those with college and/or graduate degrees, do not
remain continually in the work force from twenty-two to

sixty-five. Most of these women marry, most married women have children, and most women are ultimately responsible for the care of their aging parents. Because of these many roles, women frequently are forced to withdraw from the work force for periods of time. Many times, when they reenter, it is only on a part-time basis, and therefore they don't earn any benefits. Lots of short stints at corporations do not generate sizable pensions, if any pensions at all.

All too often, women and their husbands and families take a short-range rather than long-range view of the value of their employment. They think of it only in terms of the net dollars they bring home. They forget that the value of benefits in full-time long-term employment in a corporation can be equal to 25 percent or more of their gross pay. In forgoing the opportunity to participate in a pension plan and other benefits, women shortchange themselves. A woman at home is supposedly not only the best but the cheapest form of child care, housekeeping, business entertaining to support one's husband, and care for aging parents. If this were scrutinized a little more closely, though, it would be obvious that women lose out in a major way when they don't pay into Social Security or a pension plan or become eligible for other benefits customarily available to men who work full time, uninterrupted.

....

Take advantage of as many retirement packages as possible, even if you must pay for them yourself.

....

For those who do earn pensions, they will be one of two types: defined benefit or defined contribution. Defined benefit plans, once the most common in large corporations, are usually funded entirely by the employer. Employees are assured of a predetermined benefit upon retirement, usually in the form of monthly checks. The amount of those checks is for the most part determined by the number of years the employee worked for the corporation and the employee's earnings. Most such pension funds are conservatively invested to protect this retirement income.

Defined contribution plans are entirely different. These usually require both an employee and employer contribution and generally depend on the company's profits and losses. For this reason, it is impossible to know, until one's retirement, exactly how much is available. Retirement payments for this type of plan are generally made in a lump sum, although other payment plans can be negotiated by the employee.

It's important to check to be sure that your pension plan qualifies as tax exempt under IRS provisions. It's also important to check to see if your plan is integrated or nonintegrated. If it is integrated, your plan will only pay the amount agreed upon less your actual Social Security payments.

401-K PLANS

Some companies, especially smaller and newer ones that have no formal pension plan and pension administration, will offer plans such as a 401-K in which employees can contribute up to the percentage approved by the IRS. Employers may or may not make contributions, generally based on the performance of the company. While defined benefit pension plans are administered by the corporation, generally in conjunction with a bank, insurance company, mutual fund, or some other financial institution, 401-K plans can be administered by the company, an outside consultant, or the employees themselves.

ERISA

ERISA is the Employment Retirement Income Security Act and it protects employees in a number of ways. It establishes that employees can join a pension plan at age twenty-one and that the maximum period an employee can be forced to wait before becoming eligible for such a plan is three years. It further guarantees that all employees are entitled to full pension after no more than fifteen years. Eligibility for vesting in a retirement plan begins at age eighteen. Breaks in employment of less than five years will not result in lost vesting ability.

How will you receive your retirement funds? This is an important decision and one that should be made as part of your retirement strategy. You can take your pension as a lump sum, either upon retirement, disability, or termination (in the event of your death, a lump sum would be paid to your beneficiary) or you can receive your funds in monthly or periodic payments. These may run for a lifetime (generally not more than a fixed number of years) and upon your death remaining funds would go to your estate, or you might have what's called a Joint and Survivor Annuity, where payments are made as long as you and/or your spouse are alive. Or, again, it could be limited to a fixed number of years.

All plans also allow for withdrawals under certain conditions of hardship. And finally, most pension plans permit loans at reasonable interest rates.

However you plan to take your retirement benefits, by all means check with your accountant and/or attorney first. There are frequent changes in tax laws that have a major impact on withdrawal of retirement funds, and it is important for you to be up to date so that you are not unnecessarily penalized for the method or timing of your withdrawal.

If you are contemplating divorce, be absolutely certain that any protection you assumed you would receive under your husband's pension plan is protected. This is a complicated issue, frequently litigated, that will require the input of a skilled matrimonial attorney. (And the flip side of this, of course, is that in a divorce proceeding your husband might sue you for part of your pension plan.)

IRAs

An IRA is an individual retirement account to which you can contribute up to $2,000 a year, or $2,250 for a couple if one spouse works, or $4,000 for a couple with both working. Income taxes on the savings are deferred, as is the return on your investment. However, since IRAs were established, the tax law regarding eligibility has already changed once and is currently under examination in Congress, so may change again. Regardless of the tax law, this retirement fund will remain attractive anyway. Check with your accountant or your personal banker regarding your particular eligibility.

KEOGH PLANS

A Keogh is another retirement plan, similar to the IRA, but for use only by those who are self-employed. This plan defers taxes on the contribution as well as the earnings. Again, check with your accountant to see if you are eligible and to determine how much you can contribute.

Even if you are in a corporate pension plan, I urge you to establish some retirement fund on your own as well. The money, especially if tax deferred, can grow quickly and will be there when you need it, regardless of the outcome with your corporate pension.

ANNUITIES

Basically, annuities are savings accounts operated by insurance companies that permit you to invest and have your interest compounded tax free until withdrawal. Annuities can be paid out in a lump sum at retirement or in monthly payments either for a fixed number of years or for the rest of your life. They are a conservative and safe investment for retirement, which explains their popularity, but again, when choosing any retirement investment plan, be certain to review it with your accountant, as the tax ramifications of the various plans, as well as penalities for early withdrawal, can defeat the purpose of your investment. Be sure to check the health of your chosen annuity provider in *Best's Insurance Guide*.

SOCIAL SECURITY

The American savings rate is low—extremely low when compared with the savings rates of other industrialized nations. This hurts us as a country at home and abroad, and it is particularly devastating to those facing retirement. And yet while the overall American savings rate is very low, for many women it is nonexistent. Many women, especially those without their own private source of income, have no savings, or at least none in their own name. Women who work, though, regardless of what their personal savings habits may be, do have a kind of forced savings through Social Security. Most who work pay Social Security taxes. Upon retirement, a fixed annual (in monthly checks) Social Security benefit is available to most working women for the rest of their lives.

....

Social Security should not be relied upon to provide your entire income.

....

Social Security was never intended to provide the entire support for anyone, and it generally doesn't. Even the highest Social Security payments available right now are low. On average, Social Security provides about one-third of the income of the average retired person. Of course, if you've been accustomed to earning $100,000 or $200,000 or more a year, it will in fact provide only a very tiny portion of that income in your retirement.

The Social Security Administration provides an excellent brochure entitled "Retirement," available at all Social Security offices, which describes how you pay into Social Security, who is eligible, and how you receive your Social Security payments.

A summary of the major points covered in the retirement brochure follows:

- Social Security benefits are not intended to replace all of your lost earnings upon retirement. They should supplement your pension, savings, and investments.

- In order to receive monthly cash payments from Social Security when you retire, you must have credit for a certain amount of work under Social Security.

- If you stop working before earning enough Social Security credits for payments in retirement, those credits that you have earned will be on your Social Security record and you can add to them later.

- A person who has worked for ten years can be sure that she will be fully insured for retirement benefits.

- These credits do not determine how much you will be paid but simply that you qualify for payments.

- You can start receiving retirement benefits as early as age sixty-two.

- Medicare, for which you are eligible when you start collecting Social Security payments at sixty-five, is to help you cover the high cost of health care.

- The amount of your monthly Social Security benefits in retirement is determined by the number of years you have worked and your average earnings, up to a maximum covered by Social Security.

- Once you start receiving your Social Security benefits, your payments will increase automatically as the cost of living rises.

- While you can retire as early as sixty-two, your retirement benefits will be slightly reduced, on a permanent basis, from the level you would have earned at the official retirement age of sixty-five.

- Currently the normal retirement age is sixty-five. Starting in the year 2000, however, full benefits won't be available until retirement at sixty-seven.

- In order to project your own earnings in retirement, it is essential that you refer to the tables available through the Social Security Administration. By way of example, however, if you are currently forty-five and have had average annual earnings of $48,000 or more, your monthly payment would be $1,332. If, on the other hand, you are currently sixty-five with a similar earnings picture, your monthly payment upon your retirement this year would be $975 per month.

- The benefits you receive from Social Security *may* be affected if you become eligible for a pension where your work was not covered by Social Security and you made no Social Security contribution.

- Before you can receive any payment from Social Security, you must apply for it.

- You receive all Social Security benefits due you for the year if your earnings in that year after retirement do not exceed the annual exempt amount, which, for instance, this year is $9,360 for people sixty-five through sixty-nine. If your earnings go over this exempt amount, your Social Security benefits are reduced. This applies only to earnings from employment or self-employment, and not from other funds, savings, investments, insurance, or pensions.

- If you continue working past sixty-five and delay receiving retirement benefits, a credit will increase the ultimate amount of your benefits. These increases apply up until the time you turn seventy.

- If you move out of the United States, special rules apply. Be sure to check your Social Security office.

- Part of your Social Security benefits may be taxable if your gross income exceeds the base amount currently allowed by the IRS.

- Be certain to make contact with the Social Security Administration several years before your retirement to determine how it will work for you, and be certain to apply for your retirement benefits before—preferably six months before—your retirement date.

- If you have been divorced for at least two years and were married for at least ten, you will be eligible for a portion of your former husband's benefits. As a widow you are also eligible for your husband's benefits.

- You can call or write to your local Social Security office for a copy of a questionnaire that you can fill out and return to them in order to receive a report regarding your status with Social Security, including how much you have paid into it. It is advisable to check your Social Security records every three to five years for accuracy, to aid in your retirement planning.

···

Be sure you fully understand Social Security and what you have paid into it during your working years.

···

EARLY-RETIREMENT PACKAGES

Early-retirement packages always look good. You have an opportunity, for instance, to retire at fifty or fifty-five, rather than at sixty-five. You may be eligible for what seems like a very large lump-sum amount, payable immediately, as opposed to having to wait ten or fifteen years to get it.

These plans need careful scrutiny, generally by an attorney and an accountant. Keep in mind that employers offer these plans to save money, not to give you a bonus. The chances are that the lump sum available is actually less than they would have to pay out to you in a normal retirement plan. It is also likely that the early-retirement package comes with significantly reduced or totally eliminated benefits, such as health and life insurance. Or perhaps your insurance will continue to be available, but the deductible will go from a hundred to a thousand dollars a year. Take the time to calculate what this will mean to you over several decades.

Remember that any lump-sum payment you receive is immediately taxable, at your current rate, *unless* you roll it over into an approved tax-exempt plan.

One of the old benefits of retirement funds was that they were generally made available late in life when your tax rate was diminished. If you take early retirement at the height of your earning power and are paying the maximum tax rate, you must calculate the tax consequences accordingly.

REAL ESTATE

A generation ago, it was common for recently retired people to sell the family home for an enormous profit and to use the funds for a financially carefree retirement.

Currently, that is not a viable option. As this book is being written, the real-estate market is depressed nationally, especially so in certain regions. Many people facing retirement moved in the late Seventies or Eighties and bought at the top of the market. They are fortunate indeed if their home is currently worth more than they paid for it. They're even lucky if it's worth what they paid for it. Too many people are in a situation where their primary residence, possibly their biggest asset, is worth less than what they paid for it, and even more horrifying, possibly less than the amount of the mortgage outstanding against it. In the 1980s many people fell into the trap of home equity loans. They saw their homes increasing in value and immediately took out home equity loans on top of mortgages. Many, if not most, of these people are now in a situation where they have a negative equity in their homes. Foreclosures are up, personal bankruptcies are up, and while everyone seems to agree that the real-estate market will swing back up again, it could be five, six, or seven years before home values return to what they were in the late 1980s.

RESALE VALUE OF SELECTED ASSETS

In your retirement, you may be planning to sell your boat, your silver, your art collection. Or perhaps it's your collection of baseball cards, oriental rugs, porcelain, or fine jewelry.

The value of all of the items listed above swings with great volatility as the economy swings. First of all, you probably know that the resale value of items such as boats drops significantly every year. The resale value of silver fluctuates wildly, and you may find that while you paid a premium price for the high-quality design work of a silver piece, the value of the piece might simply be for the silver itself.

Your art collection could be valued at wildly different amounts. If you bought what you liked, and enjoyed looking at it, and paid premium prices, that may turn out to be the real value of your collection. If, on the other hand, you had special knowledge or even a good eye and bought cheap, you may find that you are able to sell things at a handsome profit. Remember, though, that the main option open to you for selling your art collection is at auction, and the auction house will take a sizable percentage off the top. Of course, capital gains taxes will be due on the proceeds of such a sale as well.

The resale value of jewelry is unpredictable. While gold and precious stones will always retain major value, again you may have paid a premium price for a piece's design. In resale you are unlikely to recoup that.

In summary, collectibles in general could fund part of your retirement, but probably significantly less than you might think.

YOUR INVESTMENT PORTFOLIO

Investments in stocks and bonds have outdistanced all other forms of investment during the 1980s. If you invested carefully, with a well-run mutual fund, for instance, during the 1970s and 1980s, you may very well have more than doubled or tripled your money.

Stocks and bonds, however, are never a sure thing short term. While a well-planned, professionally managed, balanced portfolio, with the risk widely spread, will almost always perform well long term, short-term results are impossible to predict. If you invested in the 1970s and early 1980s and sold just prior to the October 1987 crash, you have done well. If, on the other hand, you got into the market just as it was climbing in the mid-Eighties and waited too long to get out, you may have been seriously hurt—possibly even wiped out. The market is down right now, the economy is shaky, and even lifetime investment professionals have no crystal ball.

....

Every woman can have investments. The key is determining which are best—and accessible—for *you*.

....

Whether you are in your thirties, forties, or even fifties, I recommend that in planning for your retirement you invest perhaps 20 to 30 percent of your available cash in a well-managed stock portfolio. Unless you have the time, inclination, and background to deal day to day with a personal stockbroker, you will unquestionably be better off with a well-managed mutual fund or possibly a family of funds. Just as your stockbroker would invest your money, at your direction, either in low-risk, moderate-risk, or high-risk stocks, you can choose a mutual fund to do the same thing. Naturally your investment strategy should match your risk tolerance. If you are risk adverse, it is foolish to invest flamboyantly. You will be much more comfortable and have greater peace of mind if you invest conservatively to match your risk tolerance. This is a matter you need to discuss at length with your broker, or to consider in selecting your mutual fund.

If you have been investing for possibly several decades and have done fairly well, these investments will probably cover up to a third of your retirement expenses. However, as with all other avenues of income in retirement, you should not become solely dependent on this one area—to do so would open you to total disaster if your portfolio suffers significantly.

If you are in your early fifties and just starting to invest for retirement, it would be a serious mistake to rely on this avenue for as much as a third of your retirement income. Since the stock market will most probably only perform well for you long term, and you could conceivably need the money within ten years, you should probably look to this area for only 15 or 20 percent of your retirement income.

Even if you could tolerate high investment risk at a younger age, it would be foolish to take such risks now. Now is the time to look for income-producing investments, conservatively managed.

Chapter 14

Retirement and Financial Planning

୭ଏ୭ଏ୭

The Rising Prosperity of America's Retirees Is Unevenly Spread

If elderly people today seem overly conservative, insecure, and fearful, there is good reason. . . . The cost of health care poses the major threat to prosperity in retirement.

Persons aged sixty-five and older have these sources of income:

Social Security, 38 percent
assets, 26 percent
earnings, 17 percent
pensions, 16 percent
other, 3 percent

Assuming a modest 4.5 percent inflation rate and a life span of ninety years, sixty-five-year-olds retiring today must nearly triple their income over the next twenty years simply to stay even.

—THE WALL STREET JOURNAL, NOVEMBER 13, 1990

Financial planning is simply a matter of orchestrating your financial life rather than reacting to it. Financial planning is not something you do once and forget about for ten years. The financial plan you lay in your twenties, thirties, or forties will be essentially useless to you in retirement.

Financial planning is so important because everything changes so fast. If you are in your fifties, you may have thought that you would finance your retirement with the money you would clear in the sale of your primary residence. Now, just when you're ready to sell, you may be unable to find a buyer because of the real-estate slump, or worse yet, you may have a negative equity because your mortgage and home equity loans exceed the value of the property.

You may have looked forward to a comfortable retirement on your husband's pension, but you may have experienced a divorce late in your marriage and been cut off from those pension funds. Or your husband's company may have gone out of business, or been acquired by a foreign buyer.

Or you may have planned to retire to your one-bedroom condominium in Florida, only to discover that you absolutely hate Florida year-round and feel totally trapped in such a small space for anything other than a short vacation. You may miss your friends, neighbors, and family, too.

....

Financial plans should be reviewed each year.

....

You may have been certain that the smart investments you made in the 1980s would pay out handsomely in the 1990s and later decades of your retirement. But then there was the 1987 crash and the 1990 recession.

You most certainly have planned to enjoy your retirement in good health. However, even a relatively minor illness such as arthritis may have rendered your retirement plans unworkable. Or your spouse may be ill. Or your elderly parents may have run out of money and decided to move in with you.

As you can see, rational, well-thought-out long-range planning done five, ten, or twenty years ago will not work for you in retirement unless it has been updated *at least annually*. Financial planning is a growing, living thing, and it works best for you when it is properly cared for.

If you have been doing annual or even semiannual financial planning all along, you would have picked up on the early signs of a real-estate slump and perhaps not re-mortgaged or taken out that home equity loan.

Your financial plan might have included setting up a fund for the care of your parents, should that become necessary.

Your financial plan would have reflected the reality of the tenuousness of some pension and profit-sharing plans.

Your financial plan would have spread the risk in your investments so that the stock market crash of 1987 would not have wiped you out.

Your financial plan always would have included a six-month liquid contigency fund for emergencies, such as illnesses or other unexpected events.

Whatever your age at this time, it is essential that you begin formal financial planning immediately, if you haven't already done so. If you have done so (probably with your accountant) but you haven't updated your plan, you should get into the habit of annual reviews and revisions, or better yet, semiannual reviews.

Your financial plan defines your short-term and long-term goals and then defines the means by which you will achieve them.

SHORT-TERM GOALS

Your short-term goals include such things as paying the rent, paying the mortgage, paying the tuition, handling day-today living and maintenance expenses, saving, purchasing adequate insurance, setting aside a six-month contingency fund.

You need to start with a budget. Itemize all of your fixed monthly and annual expenses. Then itemize the funds available to you to cover these expenses, such as salary, commissions, dividends, interest, and/or rent paid to you.

You have positive cash flow if you have more money coming in than going out, after taxes. If your cash flow is negative and you are carrying a significant amount of installment debt, your first priority is to bring your budget into line—in other words, to balance it. Debt is expensive, and you should look first to reduce or eliminate it. Then you should look at the amounts you are spending on such fixed items as insurance, mortgage or rent, automobiles, food and clothing, and entertainment. Scrutinize each category to make sure you are getting the maximum value and that you are not overspending.

Next, you need to look at the revenue side to make sure that you are maximizing funds available to you. If, for instance, you have money in a bank savings account, where it is earning minimal interest, switch it to a money market fund. If you have investments whose performances are lackluster (they haven't moved in years), get rid of them. If the terms of your mortgage are not advantageous and you feel you could do better at another bank, move the mortgage. If you are funding two or three automobiles when you only need one, cut back.

Analyze your insurance needs. (For a more detailed discussion on insurance, see page 101.) The chances are excellent that you have too much life insurance, inadequate health insurance, and no disability insurance. Meet with a broker to review your real needs and the alternatives open to you to cover them.

....

It is always important to set goals, analyze them, and prepare contingency plans.

....

If you have an elderly parent living with you and are paying for a full-time companion, consider senior day care, which may be more appealing to your parent anyway and will certainly be considerably less expensive (assuming your parent is in good health).

If you are carrying the complete cost of a weekend house but find that you really only use it during the summer, sell it and invest the money, then rent for the summer. In this down real-estate market, you may find that you aren't able to sell it for the amount you want; still you will be free of the expense of maintaining the house, and there are many very desirable rentals available at this time.

You will probably be very pleasantly surprised when you review your budget for areas that could benefit from revision. You probably are spending too much in several categories and maybe neglecting important areas such as insurance and your contingency fund and regular savings.

Remember, inflation is now eating away at your money at the rate of anywhere from 4 percent to over 6 percent per year. Your money has to actually be earning that much just to stay even.

If you have a spouse, live-in companion, or older child living at home, repeat the planning process for them and then combine your two plans where desirable.

LONG-TERM GOALS

Now is the time to turn your attention to long-term goals, which could include the purchase of a house, college tuition for your children, funding your retirement, caring for your aging parents, starting your own business, or whatever you like.

For each long-term goal, decide how many years you have to achieve it and the amount of money it will require in the first year as well as on an ongoing basis. For instance, you may wish to buy a house in five years, which is going to require a down payment of $50,000 and then monthly mortgage payments of $2,500. Or you may be sending your child to college in ten years and expect to require $100,000 for that four-year period, one-quarter of it in the first year. You can estimate how much you need to start saving and investing at this point, and how much interest your investment will need to earn, to produce the funds required in the first year for each of your long-term goals.

Not surprisingly, you most probably cannot see at this point how you will fund all of your goals. Therefore you need to prioritize and start with the most important goal and possibly eliminate those that are optional.

All of your calculations need to be based on your current earnings and your prospects for future earnings. It is foolish to base these projections on some kind of imagined windfall down the line which may never materialize.

The majority of people find they are unable to finance their retirement when it actually comes time to retire. Very few people lay adequate plans or invest and save enough. Many people simply retire too early.

Suppose you are fifty-two and have *been* retired early. The first thing you should do is look to find other employment to bring in the funds necessary to support you until the time when you are unable or unwilling to work. That age is likely to be closer to seventy. These are now the years when you have to invest and set aside the funds for that time, for even if you do retire at seventy, your life span might be eighty-five or ninety.

We have already covered a number of options in the "Retiring onto Something" chapter, but it is important to remember that the first thing you should do in planning for retirement is pare back your budget to the bare-minimum necessities. Reduce or eliminate whatever debt you can. Look at any real-estate holdings as your potential retirement home or the means by which you will ultimately fund a new retirement home. If you've been living in an extremely expensive metropolitan area because of your previous full-time employment but now find that you will be working at home, or part time, or in the suburbs, by all means get rid of your expensive metropolitan dwelling and the surrounding expenses, unless you would find it emotionally impossible to live elsewhere. For most people, it's the other way around. They have lived near work to make the commute bearable and welcome the opportunity to live in a less expensive, less populated, and nearby area, if practical.

Be realistic about your minimum requirements for housing, transportation, food and clothing, medical expenses and insurance. Remember, this is a bare-essentials plan, and if you can embellish it later, terrific.

Once you have listed your likely expenses, itemize revenue you know you can depend on such as:

- Your monthly Social Security payment

- Pension plan payout from your former employer

- 401-K payouts

- Profit-sharing payout from your former employer

- Insurance annuity payments

- IRA payments

- Keogh payments

Use conservative estimates for your return on any investments.

Now calculate the difference between the revenues upon which you feel you can rely and the minimum required per year. For purposes of this exercise, calculate your retirement as a twenty-year scenario. You will now have the sum required, during year one and later years. It is now your task to earn, save, and invest an amount that will produce the money you need.

You actually have several options. You can work long hours now at the maximum pay you are able to earn in your profession and do nothing after age seventy, or you can cut back somewhat now and plan to continue working beyond age seventy, or you can work part time now and experiment with starting a small business, which you could work at after your retirement for as long as you wished.

Whatever your final decision, a well-thought-out financial plan now will greatly increase the likelihood of your ability to retire in the fashion you choose, when you choose.

ESTATE PLANNING

Estate planning is a key part of any retirement plan. To be more precise, revising and updating your estate plan should be a key part of your retirement plan. Estate planning should begin when you first start working. Nevertheless, a lot of people put it off as long as possible. This is ridiculous. You will have worked hard all of your life, and you should be the person to choose how your assets are managed and distributed upon your death.

....

**Estate planning will eliminate mismanagement
of your assets.**

....

The first step is to draw up a will.

The purpose of your will is to set forth in great detail how you want your assets and personal matters, including the upbringing of your children, handled in the event of your death.

Before you start, make a list of your assets. You will no doubt be surprised at how long the list is.

Next, make a list of existing debts and the method in which they should be paid.

Next, specify in detail any guardianship arrangements applicable for your children, especially if your spouse is dead or if you are divorced and you have custody of your children. You need to select the type of guardian (preferably someone very similar to yourself in age, lifestyle, education, and religion) you want to have put in charge of your children, and you must specify your wishes regarding their health care, education, religious upbringing, and social environment.

If you own your own business, you must outline how you want the business managed, or if you want it sold and the assets distributed to your beneficiaries.

Consult with your attorney and accountant in preparation of your will so that you minimize, wherever possible, the tax implications of your actions for your beneficiaries.

Specify your desired funeral arrangements.

Finally, you must select an executor or coexecutors. The job of the executor is difficult, frequently thankless, and for the most part unpaid. Your executor or coexecutors should be people with whom you've shared a close personal relationship, which will lead them to carry out your wishes rather than handle things the way they might prefer. If you have coexecutors, it's useful to have one of them be a family member and the other your personal attorney or banker.

In your estate planning, you have two main objectives: first, to provide for your dependents (both children and adults), and second, to make gifts of your choice to selected beneficiaries.

If you have three children, a spouse, a business partner, and aging parents, you will not want to simply treat them all the same and divide things six ways. You need to look at the long-range needs of your children. Perhaps one is grown and independent, one is disabled, and one is very young. Perhaps your spouse is partially disabled. Perhaps your parent or parents are in a nursing home. Once you ascertain your real net worth, distribute your assets in the best possible way to protect the needs of your dependents once you are gone. For instance, your older independent child wouldn't be likely to require as much protection as your middle disabled child. The needs of your parent in a nursing home might be very clear and easy to ascertain. The needs of your spouse, on the other hand, especially if you expect that he will remarry, could be quite complicated to deal with.

It works best to prepare a worksheet for each of your dependents, list the needs you hope to meet, and then list the assets you would like to assign to that purpose.

Once that is completed, if you have remaining assets that you wish to bequeath to friends, business associates, and/or charities, that is the relatively easy part. All of those gifts will be appreciated, but are perhaps not critical to the existence of the parties.

If you have completed your estate planning with the care outlined above, you will quickly see the importance of updating it at least annually to address changing circumstances. You will want to update it even more frequently if one of your dependents' health or financial status changes drastically.

CONSULT THE PROFESSIONALS

When you decide to tackle the issue of your retirement in earnest, you would be wise to seek out the help of a number of professionals. These include your attorney, stockbroker (or mutual fund manager), banker, insurance broker, real-estate broker, financial planner and/or accountant. You may already have a working relationship with all of these experts, but if you don't, the best way to find them is through personal references. Seek out the advice of three or four of your friends and then personally interview those people whom they recommend. The important point to keep in mind in dealing with all of these professionals is that your relationship with them is likely to be long and personal, and in addition to seeking people with good references, you will certainly need ones with whom you feel comfortable and with whom you get along.

....

Professional advice is important, but you must feel comfortable and confident with the adviser you choose.

....

Your Attorney

You probably already have a relationship with an attorney, even if it has just been to draw up your will and to review legal documents such as leases, car loans, and mortgages. If you have not reviewed your will in the last several years, you should do so at this time and possibly draw an entirely new one to reflect your circumstances as you retire. If your legal matters are going to remain relatively simple, you need look no further than the attorney you've dealt with thus far. If, on the other hand, you plan to start your own business or make some other significant change in your life that involves specialized legal documents, you would be better off using an attorney who deals in that specific area (business start-ups, for instance).

Your Accountant

Perhaps you've used an accountant for many years whose sole function has been to prepare your annual tax return and possibly to offer a little tax-planning advice. In planning for retirement, you need much more from your accountant. You and your accountant should review your current financial status and your projections for income and expenses in retirement. If your accountant is not qualified to handle sophisticated financial planning, you would do well to speak to a certified financial planner, who most probably will be an accountant also. A financial planner accustomed to structuring and monitoring retirement plans would be your best choice.

Your Real-Estate Broker

Even if you have no intention of selling your house and relocating, it is helpful to get a new appraisal on any real estate you own from a trusted real-estate broker. If it is your plan to sell your primary residence, buy a second vacation or retirement home, or buy investment real estate, you most certainly need a strong relationship with an experienced real-estate broker.

Your Banker

You have no doubt had a relationship with one or more banks all of your adult life, if only to handle your checking and savings accounts. Banks can do much more for you, and you should certainly meet with your personal banker (who will be either the person you met with initially to open your account or an officer assigned to you at a later date whose name generally appears on your monthly statement) and review the services available at your bank.

Your Stockbroker or Mutual Fund Manager

You are aware that you need to invest your available money at a rate greater than the annual inflation rate in order to simply stay even. You may be a sophisticated investor and handle your own investments with a trusted stockbroker. It is far more likely, however, that you do not have the necessary expertise and have chosen to invest through a mutual fund, thereby spreading your risk and benefiting from professional portfolio management. Just because you're planning to retire, you cannot let up on your monitoring of your investments. Your money needs to continue to grow during your retirement and, in fact, you will most probably be more dependent on your investments in retirement than you were when you were employed full time.

Your Insurance Broker

The chances are excellent that you do not have an insurance broker, but you should. You may have entrusted your insurance to your employer and/or spouse, but it is important in planning your retirement that you seize control of this critical area. As mentioned above, the best way to find an insurance broker is through personal recommendations from trusted friends or acquaintances. You also can call your local insurance board for the listings of qualified people in your area, as well as for some of the ground rules concerning the relationship between you and a broker. Since your insurance may have been provided by others in the past, you will especially want to investigate how your broker earns his or her fees on policies that you acquire.

ELIMINATE DEBT

Debt is the wild card in your retirement planning. If you are in your forties, plan to be rid of your debt (excluding your mortgage) by age fifty. If you are in your fifties, force yourself to stop buying and start to aggressively retire your debt. Although it's hard to imagine in your early earning years, you most probably will hit a point where your income stops growing. You might continue to receive small raises, but perhaps they are less than enough to make up for the annual bite of inflation. Or worse yet, once you reach your fifties, you may find yourself dead-ended at your corporation. While you may not be hit with the loss of your job or early retirement, it is in fact likely that the tremendous growth you might have seen in your salary over the last two decades will come to a halt. This means that even many years before your official retirement, it will grow increasingly difficult for you to cover your fixed expenses, such as mortgage, utilities, taxes, automobile maintenance, child care, and tuition. While it's always possible to do some belt tightening and cut back in certain areas, personal debt such as credit card or bank debt cannot be cut back in any way other than paying it off and not incurring new debt. Remember that there is no way you will be able to handle the significant drop you are almost certain to experience in your retirement income if you have not squared away your personal debt. It is even worth taking extreme steps such as the sale of a second home, a boat, a car, or a piece from an art collection. You want to be in the best possible financial shape when you face retirement. Don't burden yourself with a lot of questionable or even unnecessary debt that you are forced to carry over into your retirement.

ALLOW FOR INFLATION

The impact of inflation alone on your financial security in retirement is reason enough to become involved in personal financial planning.

When you are gainfully employed, and your salary keeps increasing, and your health is perfect, and the future looks bright, it is very difficult to force yourself to think about the impact of inflation on retirement. Inflation is bad enough prior to retirement, in that it eats away at the value of your money at the rate of maybe 4, 5, even 10 percent a year. This unpleasantness is cushioned by your increasing salary. In retirement, however, inflation continues to do its evil work while your sources of income will probably become fixed (with the exception of Social Security, which has built-in cost-of-living increases). By way of example, perhaps you now earn $75,000 a year and you have determined that you will need $50,000 per year in retirement. Perhaps Social Security will provide about $15,000 of that. The rest will be provided by a monthly annuity check, by IRA withdrawals, by cashing in an insurance policy, and by the profit you foresee in selling your primary residence. Unfortunately, all of these monies are static and simply lose their value as they sit there not working for you. In order for any of these funds to continue to throw off enough to maintain your lifestyle, you must reinvest this money in such a way that it earns in interest an amount equal to or greater than the inflation bite you experience each year.

What this all means is that you must continue to earn on

your investments in your retirement. While you certainly won't want to do anything terribly risky, you will need to put your capital in safe investments that produce the kind of retirement funds you need, whether it's certificates of deposit, Treasury bills, money market funds, or conservatively managed mutual funds.

Retirement Is to Enjoy

With careful planning, including the analysis of short- and long-term goals, estate planning, consultation of the professionals, eliminating debt, and keeping an eye on inflation, you can successfully plan the financial scenario for your retirement.

But you should also give careful consideration to the social, psychological, and physical aspects of your retirement as well. If you do, whether you decide to be a pensioner, a world traveler, a volunteer, or the president of your own organization, retirement can and should be what you have spent the first fifty years of your life looking forward to and the last fifty years of your life enjoying.

Index